HOW WE GOT HERE

THE WOMEN OF WRITELIFE

CATHY DEL NERO

JANET SKINNER

MARY CLARE O'GRADY

IRENE M HUBBARD

JUDITH PORTER, CO-EDITOR

DIANNE ELLIOTT, CO-EDITOR

JACK GALVIN, EDITOR

Publisher's Information

EBookBakery Books

Author contact: writejack33@hotmail.com

ISBN: 978-1-953080-02-8

© 2020 by Jack Galvin

ABOUT WRITELIFE

Twelve years ago, I wanted to offer a class on memoir writing for Salve Regina University's Circle Of Scholars program. I had an idea that writing The Story of One's Life might be an overwhelming task. But recalling and writing about one's most memorable stories might be manageable. The Circle of Scholars administrators liked the idea and WriteLife was born.

Students had no idea what they were in for: Write a 4-6 page paper on an assigned topic about life experience for each of seven weeks, make copies for the group (usually 6 or 7), then read the paper aloud for commentary,

Intimidating? At first. But the sharing of past experiences—on paper—brought people together. And now all these years later, after four different versions, WriteLife is still going strong as you will see for yourself as you read the essays from the women of WriteLife.

Jack Galvin

Contents

Introduction

Six women, whose backgrounds differ by age, marital status, socio-economic background, and place of birth within the United States, came together to focus on one goal: writing our story.

We found our way to the WriteLife memoir writing class in the Circle of Scholars adult seminars at Salve Regina University in Newport, Rhode Island. Our intentions for seeking out this particular genre varied from continued writing from other memoir seminars to sitting down for the first time to put-to-page our own stories.

The class offered a welcoming, supportive environment set by our teacher, who led by example and identified value in our earliest attempts to put our life's narratives into a black and white reality on a piece of paper-an oftentimes terrifying transition.

Whether it be to document a family emigration story from another country, or to illuminate how our heritage as Americans can differ by region of our vast country, or to try and exorcise some demons from the family chest of secrets: all were accepted as valid motivation by this small brave group of explorers into the brave new world of disclosing our intrinsic inheritance.

How We Got Here celebrates our inherent strength in looking into our individual, yet collective life legacies. In doing so, we illuminate how our ghosts, even subconsciously, allow us to find the path to the collective space where we all were brave and valid for wanting to bring our voices into the air.

Dianne Elliott, August 2020

PHOENIX RISING

Where The Heart Is

Cathy Del Nero

NINE YEARS OLD AND UNAWARE that my parents' marriage was deteriorating, I found great peace in being in my house. I often have dreams set in that house even now.

It was a large grey Victorian, one of many stately homes in a kid-filled neighborhood. It was on the corner of French and Belmont Streets in the Old Highlands of Fall River, Massachusetts, and was divided into two very large sunny apartments. We lived on the first floor, as had my mother in her youth, after her family was forced to sell their big house in Brooklyn. That was when they moved themselves and my Papa's lamp factory to this manufacturing town. Life here was far less expensive. She always missed New York, she would say.

Now married to a wrong husband and sentenced to stay in a wrong home in a wrong city, she bravely redecorated in shades of apricot and teal and grey, with beautiful mid-century modern furniture and dramatic artwork on the walls. It was special and so different from anyone else's house, it seemed. Our friends and hers always admired it. I loved it there. I think she grew tired of it.

I could see that my father no longer slept in the big bedroom with my mother, but in the den, which doubled as his office. I really didn't know why. In that little room, there were papers strewn everywhere. The couch, now

Dad's bed, was never neatly made each morning, as my sister and I were told to do in our room. On the floor sat a heavy, black adding machine with raised keys and a big handle to be pulled back and forth, and a roll of paper to keep record of the sums calculated. He let me play with it when he was home, which wasn't often.

There was a television in there, too. He would watch it late into the night when he finally came home, and sometimes on a weekend afternoon with my sister or me, before he went out again. He didn't travel for work. Dad just golfed and gambled and played contract bridge, ignoring his liquor store and his wholesale business, both bought for him by my mother's well-intentioned father. He simply led a life separate from Mom, Laurie, and me. It didn't seem odd then. It just was the way it was.

Our house was filled with books. Though we had bookcases in most every room, my mother had gotten some bookshelves built along the long hallway from her bedroom to the kitchen. This was done after she finished her master's degree in English and started teaching at Rhode Island College. She had to get a job after bill collectors started pounding at our heavy, oak front door in the early mornings, waking my sister and me in our shared bedroom. Mom would shout at them to go away, but they came back each week until she realized she needed to earn her own money and got a teaching position at the college. Being an English instructor appealed to her, though it required hiring a housekeeper to be home for us most days.

She had so many courses to teach (and so many more books related to them) that the new shelves filled up in no time. Though they further darkened an already sunless hallway, I was thrilled. She often asked my sister and me to read the many volumes of stories and poems she brought home from school, in order to get our opinion, she said, for her Children's Literature class. We devoured them, always looking for more, always assured that our critiques were valuable.

Our living room was double sized with a baby grand piano on one end and a beautiful black marble fireplace on the other. In front of the oversized nine foot couch, which faced the fireplace, was a black marble coffee table from Italy. It had streaks and swirls of white and brown ingrained in the shiny black stone, and it matched the sides of the fireplace and the hearth. I own that table now and cherish it. It was a stable to my toy horses, a dollhouse to Laurie's Barbie dolls, and a hiding place under which our dog, Fitzy, slept when we would finally stop annoying him.

In the corner of the living room, to the left of the fireplace next to a window, was a wonderful gold and cream patterned high back armchair and a matching ottoman. It was my seat of choice in the evenings or afternoons. I would curl up in it anytime I could get there before my sister did and read my two-books-from-the-library and one-from-Adam's-Bookstore, where my mother took us early every Saturday morning. I loved being in that chair, in that spot, looking up and out of the window occasionally, keeping tabs on any neighborhood pals who might be outside, starting a game of kickball or dodge ball in the street. I was in that chair on a November Tuesday in 1965 around 5:30 pm, home alone, waiting for my sister and mother to return from shopping, when the lights went out in The Great Northeast Blackout. Halfway through *Gone with the Wind*, I was suddenly in total blackness, not a streetlight nor a porch light visible anywhere. The neighborhood was dead silent, yet I was oddly unafraid, comfortable sitting there, seeing only familiar dark grey shapes outside and inside, in the blackness.

On Sundays, I had a favorite job. Given money and the authority to pick up our Sunday newspapers from Murray's Drug Store, I would grab my shiny black English three-speed bicycle from the shed in back of the house and ride a mile or so to New Boston Road. There I would pick up the copies of the *New York Times*, the *Boston Globe* and the *Boston Herald* that were saved for us, pay at the soda fountain, and ride proudly back home with the papers in the basket attached to the handlebars.

My mother immediately would take possession of the *New York Times Sunday Magazine*, replete with crossword puzzle, and sit at the kitchen table for a couple of happy hours. I would bring the sports sections into the den, and either deliver them to, or leave them for, my father. Laurie would greedily grab the front sections of each paper as well as all of the comic strips, which we called "funnies", and retreat to her desk in our bedroom.

Left to myself, I secretly took the *Boston Herald* middle section, which each Sunday had a long article describing a hideous rape and murder. I would lie belly down on the living room carpet near the fireplace, staring at grisly black and white pictures of the lovely young women who had been savagely killed. I would read the articles slowly, the type small and the story so long and awful, that I would scare myself to death. I told no one I did that. If anyone walked by me, I flipped the page and pretended to be skimming some other story or fashion ad, fooling my family and keeping my horror to myself. It was my secret, though I will never understand why I did this week after week. When I finished the article, my hands were filthy from the newspaper ink, and my mind equally soiled from the content.

We stayed in that house till I was fourteen years old, and my parents finally separated. My father would not move out, even after the house was sold and the movers had taken away all of my mother's and my sister's and my things. Finally, the day before the new buyers were to move in, my sister and I were sent to the house, charged with trying to urge him to get a truck to take away his belongings. He would not listen, and remained stubbornly holed up in the den, with his papers and adding machine and television. Joined now by his suitcases, crammed with all of his clothes.

I couldn't bear seeing the house emptied of all but him and some furniture my mother left for him, including my beloved reading chair sitting alone near the window. My sister went to call my mother for further instructions.

And I stood in the empty living room and wept.

MISCALCULATION

CATHY DEL NERO

I AWOKE TO A FAINT BUT persistent clanging. My eyes were stuck shut, and I could not breathe through my nose. I opened my mouth and took in some air. My throat was so sore.

I pulled at my crusted eyelashes, finally managed to blink, and realized my head hurt and my body ached.

My sister, waking now in the bed on the other side of the room we shared, turned on the light and finally got the alarm clock to stop its noise. She glanced over as I sat up slowly and swung my legs over the bed's edge to the pink linoleum floor. It felt cold and so did I.

Laurie looked at me and shook her head. "You're a mess. You must have caught a cold. Better tell Mom you're staying home."

"You gave me this," I muttered. "I told you to keep away. Can't stay home. Have lesson on the slide rule today." Talking hurt.

Seventh grade math with Mr. Demetrius, who said Laurie was the best student he had ever had. A lot to live up to with my competitive spirit. My sister, 15 years old, and so smart, was a hard act to follow. If she knew how to use a slide rule, well so was I. So I slipped down the hall as she looked for her robe, and I got into the bathroom first, avoiding the holdup from her daily makeup and hair routine. Ninth grade demands of eyeliner and mascara were her morning religion. I spent the next five minutes blowing my nose and putting cold water on my hot face and eyes. I brushed my teeth and winced. That hurt too.

At the breakfast table fifteen minutes later, dressed and weary, I sat waiting for my mother to put whatever breakfast she had made in front of me. Scrambled eggs and toast appeared. She was dressed in her maroon suit and matching high heels, looking sharp, ready to take on college freshmen in "Kiddie Lit" at Rhode Island College. She put her cool hand on my forehead.

"You're warm and look pretty awful. Laurie's cold, I guess."

Laurie glared at us both from her seat opposite, in her on-going role as arrogant teenager.

"You want to stay home today, Honey? Dad is sleeping still."

"Nope." I said using as few words as possible. "Slide rule today."

"Okay then. Eat your eggs. I'll get you something."

Her heels clicked on the floor as she went into the small bathroom, opened the medicine cabinet, and returned with a blister pack of four capsules. She broke out two of them. I read the word *Contac* on the silver foil.

I had never taken these before. But Laurie had the week before when she was sick. I presumed I had some-how matured by being offered this adult medication, so I swallowed two with my now-tasteless orange juice. They went down with some resistance in my swollen throat, but I didn't let on. I put the other two in my pocket as I took the lunch bag from my mother, who kissed my head and not my face. I totally got it.

A short while later I was walking, mostly following, my self-pronounced glamorous sister down Belmont Street to Morton Junior High School of Greater Fall River, a mile away. Usually the walk was a highlight of my day. Ours was a neighborhood of fine old Victorian houses with beautiful trees and lovely gardens. Though there were still some orange and yellow leaves stuck to the branches, most were on the sidewalk, slippery now from the rain of the night before. Generally I loved the smell of the chestnut pods cracked open, spilling their nuts onto the sidewalk, and the odor of wet bark and steamy sidewalks after an autumn shower. Today I smelled none of that and was miserable lugging my backpack stuffed with books and feeling my nose, just stuffed, down the slippery hill.

Laurie got far ahead toward the last block by North Park, so as not to be seen as related to the scruffy, snuffling mess following her. I didn't care. My nose did start to dry up, probably due to the pills I thought. But I felt odd. Light-headed. Definitely not feeling too social, I smiled weakly and waved as I walked past some friends and got to my homeroom shortly before the bell sounded, seemingly very far away. I made it through some morning classes, my fever lessened, swollen glands a bit less painful, and my blocked nose and crusted eyes seemingly undetected by my teachers and pals. My ill humor was not. The "Two Susan's" and the other of the "Two Cathy's", who were my longtime best buddies, avoided me, guessing I was both contagious and ill humored. Right they were.

Lunchtime. I dropped to a chair in the cafeteria, away from anyone I knew. I saw my sister at the far end of the room. She looked up and our eyes met for a moment. But she turned a disgusted face away from me in order to return to chat with her many friends at their cool-kids table.

For me, lunch consisted of opening up the brown bag Mom had handed me before I left home, pulling out the sandwich I could not consider eating, and finally getting up slowly, to drop it into a trash receptacle nearby. My usually welcome cookies and a red apple followed. I stared into the rubbish for a while, not wanting to look up, not wanting to sit down, not actually wanting anything, but merely being content to be still in one place while the room wobbled a bit. Finally a lunch lady shooed me away as she glanced into the waste can, shaking her head at my personal waste of a perfectly good lunch.

As I shuffled out of the green-walled and noisy lunch area, I stopped at the bubbler, reached into my pocket, and pulled out the foil packet with the remaining two cap-sules. My nose was tingling again, and I thought I had better take them now, before my math class, to try to keep both nose and eyes from running endlessly. I put them in my mouth, gagged a bit, but they went down my reddened and irritated throat. Up the stairs to the second floor I went, thinking every step was my last.

The door was open to Mr. Demetrius' classroom. I ducked inside before he, as well as my schoolmates, arrived. I was generally a good student and had always exhibited some interest in math. Mr. Demetrius liked me, and I thought he was kind. But today I took the unusual step of sitting in the last row, thinking I would be some-how invisible there. It seemed to work, as only a couple of the usual bad boys seemed to follow me back there. But though they scowled at my intrusion, they too could tell they should stay away, so they seated themselves a few rows to my right. There was a movie projector ahead of us in the middle of the classroom.

"Okay guys," said Mr. Demetrius, as he entered, closing the classroom door behind him.

The clock above his head on the wall showed it was 12:20. He passed out a bunch of slide rules to a couple of kids in the front, who handed them backwards through the rows. I put mine on my desk. It looked complicated. The seemingly thousands of intricate lines and tiny numbers and weird marks on it looked fuzzy. And part of the ruler slid forward and back. It was all dizzying to my already spinning mind. Mr. Demetrius lowered the lights and pointed to a small movie screen he'd set up in the front of the room.

"This is it. Slide Rule Day. Pay attention. Watch the film. No talking. You need to learn this material and learn it well if you plan to multiply, divide, and calculate some big problems going forward. If you plan to pursue math and take Trig in high school, this is the only way you'll get there."

He held up the slide rule as if to make this point, started the projector, and there on the screen was a model of the same slide rule as was on my desk. I stared in confusion at the giant tool and propped my warm chin on my hand. I could barely focus.

A deep voice began to explain, "The slide rule is an instrument that was used to design virtually everything. Its size ..."

A hand shook my shoulder gently but firmly.

"Cathy. Hey. What's wrong? Hey".

I lifted my head from the desktop. I touched my now burning cheek and felt the impression of the slide rule on which I had slept.

I looked up at Mr. Demetrius, who was looking at me with some concern and a fair bit of amusement. I could hear some muffled giggles. I looked at the clock. 1:03 it said. I looked back at my teacher.

"*Contac*", I attempted to say. But my stuffed nose and sore throat made it sound like gibberish.

"Go to the office and tell them I said to send you home. You're sick," he said firmly.

"Slide rule," I whispered, ashamed and exhausted as I gathered my books and shuffled out of the room.

My mother was already home from her class and picked me up. Twenty minutes later, I was in my bedroom, wearing my soft, green nightgown. and was tucked into bed.

"*Contac*," I mumbled seriously to my Mom, as she moved toward the door. I don't think she knew what I said.

"Slide rule," I tried next. She shook her head. I fell asleep.

Sometime later, I awoke in the dark, feeling a bit woozy. Fever down some. Still congested. I could see my sister was not in the room and her bed was made. The silent clock said 7:30.

"Oh no!" I thought. "I'll be late for school!"

I got dressed quickly, ran to the bathroom and drew a comb through my hair. I sat down at the kitchen table. Laurie was nowhere to be seen.

My mother was at the stove. She turned and said softly, "Feeling better? You hungry?"

She looked at me a bit oddly, but I thought little of it until she reached into the oven and pulled out a plate of food with foil over it.

That's odd. Looks like the way she keeps dinners warm for my father, I thought.

Then I realized Mom was wearing the same maroon skirt and blouse from the morning. That was weird. She pulled off the aluminum wrap from the plate. There was a steak, some mashed potatoes and green beans. I stared at the dish. Then I stared at my mother, and she at me. What was happening?

"Mom, it's morning. I don't want this for breakfast."

She smiled. "It's 7:30 in the evening. I think you had better go back to bed."

"*Contac*." I sputtered. "Slide rule."

"Never again," she agreed, smiling.

She was right on both counts.

Never took that stuff again.

And thankfully calculators arrived for the eighth grade.

ACORN

Cathy Del Nero

GUESSING AT MY PARENTS' PERSPECTIVE, I can only imagine that the one thing they had in common was regret. From my own, it seems clear that they had dreams that they did not share, that they simply and separately left unfulfilled. Perhaps they were so ill conceived, that they just could not realize them.

I guess Mom came closer to success over time, going back to school to get a master's degree and finally, triumphantly, her PhD in Linguistics. Education was, in her mind, the most important objective. Not unusual for a Jewish girl brought up with such culture and wealth. But her path there was not actually chosen, but more likely dictated by my father, whom she mistakenly married on the rebound, after a failed affair with a more suitable and successful fellow. Dad mismanaged his money and hers, until he finally forged her name on stock certificates, selling them and spending the proceeds, destroying her trust and her inheritance, and pushing her into the role of the 1960's highly criticized working mother. She didn't really care what people said about her working, but I was never sure she was satisfied with its being at Rhode Island College. Or in Rhode Island, at all. She sure did not like Fall River, the Massachusetts town in which we lived.

Fall River was where she and her sister and their parents had moved from Brooklyn, when the sisters were teenagers, to relocate the family business, a successful lamp factory. In New York their home had been big and grand, full of art and books and music. My mother's world had included museums and theatre and the symphony. Moving to this small and relatively uncultured place was a nightmare for her. She managed to make friends but was anxious to get back to the pace and art scene of New York, which she did by attending NYU a few years later. She returned to her family after earning her degree, met my father and married him on a whim, oddly settling for a life and a husband who were not in sync with her interests or dreams.

My father was born and raised in Fall River. His mother died when he was very young, and his father owned and ran a gas station, never remarried, and treated his children harshly. Dad graduated high school and joined the Navy toward the end of World War II. Handsome and funny, he was also quick with numbers, and got himself accepted to Brown University through the GI Bill. He then managed to "graduate early" rather than to be disciplined and expelled after an incident involving a red lantern hung on a girls' dormitory. And then he, Donald Lash, a poor and a traditionally raised young Jewish man, met and charmed and fell in love with the wealthier and avant-garde, Muriel Shapiro.

Mom's father bought Donald a liquor store to own and manage, but his son-in-law wanted a far more glamorous life. He was mesmerized by movie stars, comedians, nightclubs, gambling, and a life that was never meant to be his. My mother had no interest in any of it. Once he bought her a flashy cantaloupe-colored coat with a huge fox collar dyed to match. It neither suited her style nor her auburn hair, clashing with both. She never wore it, my sister and

I noted silently, though we did sometimes, when no one was looking.

When we were small, there were some happy times and fun with my father. He had a huge smile and a deep belly laugh and told jokes constantly. He remembered everyone's birthday and always called or sent a funny card. He taught me to do math problems in my head by calling out large numbers and showing me how to add, subtract, multiply and divide them by estimating. Often he packed endless kids into his station wagon, taking us to Red Sox games or to the circus, where we ate cotton candy and popcorn and drank soda to our hearts' content.

Yet as we got older, Dad's frustrations mounted. He wanted to play golf, not work at his store. He wanted to be rich and important. Sometimes he displayed some terrifying bouts of anger and yelled loudly at and spanked us. But he never went so far as to beat us, as his own father did him. He was always remorseful. But it scared me and was hard to forget.

He rarely raised his voice to my mother, but he treated my sister and me and sometimes others to some nasty and belittling remarks. Some would shrug off his loud and cruel words, but I could not. If he were home after we got in from school, he would call out from the den, his makeshift office and bedroom, at the far end of our home, for one of us to bring him a drink or a snack. As we got older, we were less inclined to bring our friends home if he were there, as his demands were many, and we were embarrassed at having a Dad who was home during the day and who shouted out orders from a darkened room.

My mother began to live her life separately from him, inviting colleagues from the college for drinks and dinner at our home when Dad was out at night. It seemed to me to be like the salons in French society in the 18th and 19th centuries. There were poets and painters and musicians. The conversation was electric in its intensity, a morass of politics, literary disagreements, and art critiques. And then, as words became fewer and glasses were emptied, the evening would begin to end, often with someone moving to the piano bench in order to play a classical piece on the baby grand, the chords so perfect it silenced everyone. Laurie and I were mesmerized by the glamour of it all. In those moments, my mother looked so happy and at peace, as if she were exactly where she was meant to be. She drifted further and further away from her mom-self to her academic-self, as time went on. I really missed having her more to my-self.

These two mismatched people lived in one house, but in two different worlds. My sister and I were young enough to still be immersed in the conflict, but old enough to see it was not going to end well. And it didn't. Fortunately for my sister, she was already able to drive and to have a group of friends and endless football games and dances to distract her from the messiness of two parents breaking a family apart.

Laurie mastered and maintained an ability to talk to both Mom and Dad with some adult authority, a skill learned, perhaps, from dealing with their childish behaviors. And she had with each of them a relationship quite separate from my own, though I didn't realize it for a long time. She accepted and ignored more and was less challenging to them. She didn't mind my father's shouting as I did, and to this day, she often raises her own voice herself to make a point. She is fanciful about her life, making and shaping it into a glamorous story that pleases and excites her. By age twenty-one, she had moved to Australia, a half-world away from them and also from me. Not really so different from our mother, who remarried around that same time, or our father, who wandered off to Florida. They all just removed themselves from me and from each other in so many ways.

For a short time in my younger adult years, I tried Donald's method of yelling at people when I disagreed. I scared myself and could see early on that no one else wished to hear my volume, nor listened any harder if I hollered. To this day, I hate shouting. It is frightening. The louder someone yells, the softer I speak. It works much better.

Like Muriel, I have had a career while rearing my children. In my early forties, I started to let my work life seem more glamorous than home. It lasted for a split second, until the memory of my mother's abdication came flying back and struck me hard. I realize I am far more fortunate than she was to live in a time where I do not have to suffer the stigma of a working mother. Yet while I did enjoy my career, I have always known my children are the very best part of my life, along with a husband who happily shares my values, my interests and my sense of humor.

One never entirely sheds the past, of course. I remain a champion at remembering friends' birthdays and am famously accurate when adding large sums in my head. I can recite some beautiful poetry, and I choose to listen to beautiful music.

I have lived my life with little regret. Acutely aware, of course, that acorns can be flung a pretty good distance, and yet be unmistakable products of a gnarled old tree.

COLOR-BLIND

CATHY DEL NERO

T HERE WERE NO BLACK CHILDREN at my grammar school. Nor were there any in my neighborhood at the top of the hill where I lived in relative splendor. That is if one contrasted my home to those inhabited by the larger population of my schoolmates, who lived down that steep hill in the north end of Fall River. Most of them lived in the three-decker tenement houses, in run-down apartments rented by their parents, mostly factory workers. There were no children of color there either. So when my father and Billy Weston, a black jazz musician from Newport, dropped me off at the Westall School one afternoon after my school lunch break at home, I suppose the appearance of our family friend may have seemed out of the ordinary to anyone there in the schoolyard. But it was not to me.

I grew up never hearing that black people or Asian people or Arab people were different from me. My parents simply never mentioned it. Looking back, I think it was odd for the times, the 1950's and 1960's.

Ours was a Jewish family, but we did not practice our religion in a big way. So other than my thinking Christmas was a stroke of luck gift-wise for my pals, that nuns wore scary outfits, and that churches smelled of incense not used in our temple, I just thought everyone was the same. My father had a business partner who was Lebanese. His store manager was from Portugal. My mother had colleagues from Greece and Italy. We lived in an area surrounded by neighbors who were of Irish, British, Italian, French and Canadian descent. They were Catholic and Congregationalist and Episcopalian and Presbyterian. No one in my house mentioned any differences. I figured it out later.

The first time I became aware that anyone could not like another person for simply being what he or she was, happened in the second grade at the Westall School. I was sitting by myself on an old fire escape on the side of the beat-up brick building at recess, watching my sister and her friends play dodge ball.

"Hey you. Yeah you. You're Jewish aren't you?"

I looked up to see Christine Gagnon, popular and a VIP in our class of seven-year-old's. She had three or four other girls standing just behind her, all of them staring at me. Christine's face was dead serious. But was she taking notice of me?

I smiled shyly. "Well, yes." She wants to be my friend, I thought. They all must.

"You killed Jesus Christ," she hollered, pointing at me, red-faced, with her posse nodding silently in agreement. Even the dodge ball game stopped.

"No I didn't," I replied, realizing how dumb she must be. The Victim in Question had been dead for such a very long time. What was she talking about?

I ignored her, and she finally she retreated with a toss of her head, leading the other little girls to another spot on the playground, far away from the purported murderess. I was puzzled. The dodge ball game resumed.

I was new in the neighborhood school that year, having spent kindergarten and then my first grade year, at a Baptist school. It was the only one that would take me, as I had not turned age five by the appointed date of January 1. I was the last one to go to school, and I imagine my mother was anxious to get me out of the house and have more time to herself. I could already read, thanks to my over-zealous cousins and my sister making me the only student when we played school. So off to The Christian Day School of Greater Fall River I went.

That is, until one day when I came home to my mother and announced that Headmistress Ameigh, the terrifying wife of the terrifying minister, had told me that afternoon, in a raspy whisper close to my ear, "Cathy, you will go to Hell if you do not believe in Jesus Christ."

Upon hearing this, my mother was calm, but firm. "No, Cathy, you will not go to Hell. You will go to public school."

Years later, I told her it was the same thing.

As I got older and progressed to junior high school and finally to BMC Durfee High School, I met and befriended not only kids with black and brown skin, who seemed to notice their own differences, but also Jewish kids from families to whom being Jewish was of huge significance. The kids who were of color were mostly Cape Verdean, children of Portuguese immigrants from the islands. The Jewish kids were, for the most part, from far wealthier families than mine, and all lived in the Highlands, a fancy neighborhood further north in the city. Though I made friends with a few, I didn't fit in too well with them. They went to Hebrew School every Tuesday and Thursday afternoon after school, and to services every Saturday morning at Temple Beth El. They even went to Sunday school. My mother had never thought kids should spend so much after-school time inside, and she told the Rabbi so. He didn't like it, but it suited my family just fine.

So when the Catholic and Protestant boys started to ask the Jewish girls for a date, or the Jewish boys fell for Christian girls, all hell seemed to break loose as far as I could see. I was shocked. My girlfriends were kept from their crushes and were, therefore, often in tears. That is, at least until they figured out that they could lie to their parents, waving as they drove off with a bunch of 'acceptable' kids of the same religion or color. Later they would get passed off to other cars where the boys of their current dreams waited impatiently. I finally asked my mother what the heck the fuss all was about. She explained, really for the first time, that many people actually did not like other folks of a different religion or color, simply because of that faith or skin tone. I guess I could see that, but I had a difficult time digesting the ugly information.

And then it was my turn. I fell for one of my sister's friends, a handsome, shy, popular and polite boy named Jimmy Silva. It was mutual, and we became a happy high school couple. He was a football player and a senior, to my artsy sophomore self. And he was Catholic and Cape Verdean, with coffee-colored skin. I never thought about his color or any differences. My friends did not seem to, either. My mother adored him, helping him apply and get accepted to Rhode Island College. I am not sure my father met him, as my parents had separated and divorced by then, but he certainly never expressed any concern about Jimmy and me.

In my senior year, my mother got remarried and moved to Newport, where my stepfather owned a home on Ocean Avenue. I stayed for a while with my Fall River aunts, my father's sisters, so as to be closer to school. A few months before, Jimmy had been inevitably scooped up by a classmate at Rhode Island College, causing me some temporary, teenage heartbreak. But it was not the breakup that shocked me to my core. It was one of my aunts, whom I overheard complaining on the phone to my mother about my late weeknights spent with friends or at play practice.

"She's probably out with that, that *schvartze,*" she whispered in a particularly unpleasant and hissy tone

And with that horrible Yiddish slur for a black man, she burst my innocent bubble and made me understand for the first time, that someone in my family, my own family, someone I loved, could be capable of the despicable crime of bigotry. She never knew I heard her. I made excuses and moved out.

I was seventeen, disappointed and distressed, and truly unaware of how often such nastiness was and is yet spoken. I heard what she said, and then, of course, I heard and saw a good bit more as I went to college and became an adult. Thanks to my parents, I just never have accepted such narrow-minded intolerant behavior. I still don't.

It took a long while, but I forgave my aunt, quietly in my mind. I just felt I had to.

But I will never understand. And I know I must never forget.

THE TWO OF HER

CATHY DEL NERO

I HAVE ONE SISTER. WELL, I have two sisters. That is to say I had one sister with whom I grew up, who went away. And then that one disappeared. Someone else took her place.

I was the second of two daughters, "Laurie's younger sister". That's how I was referred to at school for the first seventeen years of my life. We were two years and a world apart. Until she was fourteen and I twelve, she was quite chubby to my stick thin. She had brown hair and skin that would tan. I was blonde, and my skin only got pink, then red, then blistered in the sun. She seemed to retain every fact in every school subject, but could never remember how babies were made. I could not digest chemistry or biology, but took it upon my young self to repeat the sex talk to her each year when she returned home from summer camp. She was surprised again every August.

In those early years, we were friends at times, argued often, but laughed a lot. Having parents who were not good for or with each other, we did often look after one another. But in general, we each played and hung out with our own set of friends.

As she lost weight, caught some boys' attention, and started to date, she developed a habit of telling my mother every detail of her budding romances. I had no intention of doing that, presuming I was ever to have a love life of my own. They would talk and laugh, their heads close together at our kitchen table, but would stop if I entered the room, like conspirators planning a heist. They did not share with me what Laurie was revealing, and I didn't want to know. I was quite sure that whatever she was up to was likely over-shadowed by her habit of forgetting about the birds and the bees every year.

When Laurie left for Middlebury College, I remained at home as an only child with an only parent, the divorce and move to a soulless apartment completed. My mother continued to write her doctoral dissertation, starting a new habit of drinking heavily. She was disappointed and sad, and she missed Laurie. I missed her too, at first, but could drive by then. I managed a couple of visits to ski with her in Vermont, sleeping happily on the floor in her dorm. But soon her life there was her own, and our letters and calls were fewer, and then stopped.

So much changed so quickly. My mother met and married Alex, a Navy Captain at the War College, who had two PhDs and no intention of sharing my mother with Laurie or me ever again. I escaped to Tufts University, starting a new chapter of my own.

Laurie spent her junior year in Paris, and then the next forty plus years in Australia. She had met a veterinary student from there while skiing in Austria, and she gave up her senior year and her college degree in order to follow him back to Brisbane. He dumped her, but she fell in love with the country, with traveling, and unfortunately, with other poorly chosen men.

Within a few years, Laurie decided to become a veterinarian and applied to the University of Queensland. She was twenty-four, and her grit and her academic brilliance were on display. She easily sailed through five years of academics into a required apprenticeship set in Darwin, a tough redneck town that had been wiped out in a cyclone a few years before. After only a month or two of working in the assigned practice, she called my mother to report that the veterinarian, under whom she had apprenticed, had suffered a nervous breakdown, and that she was forced to open her own veterinary business. And that she did.

Within a couple of years she had built a practice, a surgical hospital and a country-wide reputation She purchased a farm and much land at the low interest rates offered to those who would stay in the ravaged, rough town. Laurie began to earn a huge amount of money.

She didn't come back to the United States to visit for a long time. She would phone now and then, though none of us could understand much of what she said, as she had adopted an indecipherable Australian accent. She had also gotten quite tough and sounded coarse.

After college, I spent some years sailing, cruising, and then racing yachts in the Caribbean. I met my first husband, John, a New Zealander, and we decided to get married. I did ask Laurie to be my maid of honor, but she was too busy to come back home for the wedding, she said. I wasn't surprised.

But I was startled months later, when she finally visited and asked my new husband, whom she was meeting for the first time, "Why would you marry someone so unadventurous, who has never traveled anywhere?"

He was speechless. So was I. I had lived and studied in London. And I had traveled extensively both in Great Britain and throughout Europe. In addition, I had sailed thousands of sea miles in both the Atlantic and Caribbean. And, of course, had visited John's family in New Zealand. I reminded her of all of this, but she persisted in this description of me.

This visit and those afterward would prove to be more and more difficult. I became sadly aware that she was jealous of me and my life. My husband pointed it out, but like any second child, I thought that such envy from an older sibling seemed impossible. Yet the signs were there.

It became a habit for her to make hateful comments about me to John. I tried to overlook that. A few years later, clearly annoyed when we had a child before she had thought of it, she chose to get pregnant, partnering with an ill-tempered Australian lout named Terry, whom she bullied into having a baby he clearly did not want. He left her shortly after little Marcie was born.

Laurie became somewhat obsessed with being the favorite offspring. It started with our father. I didn't mind that so much, as I found him to be more and more difficult over the years. Next she focused on my mother and her second husband, traveling the twelve thousand miles from Australia regularly to visit with them in Florida or to go on cruises with them. She did not want to visit my little family in Rhode Island anymore, or to have us join her and our parents on their trips.

Competitive about our children and our differing lifestyles, she became more and more critical of me. The divisiveness grew until finally, on a rare visit by John and me and our children to our parents' Florida home, she became physically wild in her anger. With our collective three children in attendance, she struck me, knocking me to the floor. I was both astonished and frightened. Physical violence was not something familiar to me.

I realized then that I needed to divorce myself from her. I wondered how this could have happened. My friends had loving relationships with their sisters. My own mother was close to hers. My father's sisters clung to each other. I could not make sense of it.

With no clear path to becoming an only child in my forties, I was forced to forge one. I had little contact with Laurie for years.

John was diagnosed with cancer after seventeen years of our marriage. Life was upside down for us over the next four years. As his death approached, there came a phone call from Laurie, and an offer to visit. So sure she was needed and forgetting why she was not, Laurie tried to insist on coming to help. I told her no.

Months after his death, she called again. This time it was to announce that she was getting plastic surgery to make her body tiny, her face smooth, and men more available. Overwhelmed with my own grief, I could barely listen.

Who was this person?

Sure enough, she sent pictures taken after the many operations and recuperations from the plastic surgery and follow-up skin removal that took the better part of two years. I did scrutinize them. It could have been anyone in those photos. The now blonde haired, size zero body and stretched face were foreign to me. On another phone call, she shared with me that there were many men now interested in her. But, she confided, she wanted only the younger ones, insisting that, because she looked like a forty year old, she would tell them she was that age. She was nearly sixty.

Life took a good turn when I met Paul, and a few years later we decided to marry in Florida. My mother and her sister, Enid, and their husbands lived there, aged and unwell, and could not travel. Paul thought that we should have the ceremony there for them, with my children acting as attendants for us. The plans for the wedding began. This time, Laurie made it clear she was coming.

A few days before the wedding, she arrived with her twenty-one year old daughter, Marcie, five huge suitcases, and a promise to assist us with any last minute wedding preparations. But instead of her helping us as she had offered, she surprised us with demands that we spend our time taking her to shop for sailing gear, as she had recently developed a new passion for the sport that Paul and I had enjoyed for so many years. Though busy with our own plans, we tried to keep the peace by driving her to chandleries and giving her our opinions as she asked. Every piece of our collective advice was rejected. Our heads ached.

The party the night before the ceremony and the wedding itself were small and lovely. For both events, Laurie dressed in tiny, sparkly dresses that were short and tight, causing my stepfather much enjoyment and my uncle, some despair. My mother and her sister, Enid, pretended not to notice. Laurie's daughter was stoic, and my children, amused. Paul was a bit embarrassed.

It was important to Laurie that everyone was looking at her. And we were.

Sadly, I was the one who could not recognize her.

PHOENIX RISING

CATHY DEL NERO

I USED TO HAVE WHAT I thought was a family. A mother and a father and a sister. And four aunts, two uncles, four cousins, two grandfathers, and one grandmother. Most of them have left the planet. Some have just gone missing. I'm still here, like the lone survivor in a science fiction movie after the world is blown up.

And yet I suppose each relative did give me some piece of myself. For better or worse. I accept that.

My mother instilled in me a love of books, music, theatre, and art. And she taught me to value education. But somehow she just got tired of having children, having me, and it showed. She abdicated, as a family friend observed. That was a tough one.

My father taught me to laugh. He liked to tell jokes, make up stories, and read the funnies. And he spent a lot of time drilling me on adding and subtracting large numbers in my head. And then he wandered off, bored perhaps, always looking for something more. I think it was hard for me to learn boys or understand men for a very long time.

My sister just left. I can't blame her, as she, too, experienced the same parents and lack of parenting. She went off to seek her fortune and found it thousands of miles away, becoming a stranger to me in so many ways, but an interesting acquaintance anyhow. We stay in touch now and again, but at arm's length.

Each of my parents had a sister who was ashamed of her own badly behaved sibling, and who expressed a great interest in me. I thank my lucky stars for my aunts, Enid and Doris. Without much attention from my own parents, I challenged these aunts for a long time, behaving poorly at times. But as I grew older, I saw in them so much of what I wanted to be. In Enid, I discovered the joy of philanthropy and love of the outdoors as I took note of her grace and style. Doris taught me how to look after others, to be kind to those in need, and illustrated these qualities by populating her dinner table and home with strangers who had nowhere else to go. Both of them were the flames to which my inner moth was drawn.

When I was thirty-one years old, I married John, who was born and raised in New Zealand. When he immigrated to the United States, he attracted the attention of my father's first cousin, Melvin, and his English born wife, Sheila, who each recognized what we did not: that a marriage between two people from different countries and cultures is more complicated. They shared with us their own successes and mistakes, and, with that, they became surrogate parents to us both. They offered their advice and their time, as I had always imagined a mother and father would do. We shared a love of boats and books, and life was just so much easier with them in it.

Over the next few years, John started a graphic design business, and continued his love of racing sailboats in the bay. I got my financial planning career started. We bought a house, adopted our two children, and began our life as a family, though neither of us had a clue how to do that.

Being a mother came naturally to me, though bearing children had not. I loved it. Being a wife was foreign to me. I knew little of family life. I was startled to realize that I hadn't had one.

Only now do I see the mistakes John and I made. We spent a lot of time apart, forgetting to reserve some for ourselves as a couple. We argued in front of the children. We didn't discuss our finances; we fought about them. John did not accept that a wife could make more money than a husband, and he didn't like it. And I didn't see how easy it could be to try to soften that blow. I had no experience with parents who talked things out, who worked together. That is the detritus of my own family's chaos.

Where all of this might have taken me, taken John, taken all of us, I will never know. In early 2002, he was diagnosed with a rare cancer in his sinus, and we began a sad journey for four years, navigating our way through radiation, chemotherapy, and horrendous and cruel surgeries on his face and mouth. There was no time for us to better learn to be a family or a couple. The days were filled with kids moved here and there and doctor's appointments and trips to Boston and back home. My plan to make a better life, a better family for my children was under attack.

John died in our bed upstairs in our beautiful home, which he had lovingly designed. It was on a Sunday evening in late January of 2006, and no surviving member of my family of origin was present but me.

This was hardly a shock, as none of them had visited in any of the four years prior, either. Not when John's cancer first was diagnosed, nor while it ebbed and flowed, unchecked. They were simply not there to comfort my kids or me as we watched him disintegrate before our eyes.

In the room where John quietly took his leave were the real family members, the family of friends one gathers and creates lovingly and luckily, out of need. Sheila, now Auntie

Sheila to the children and anyone else we met, was there as well, in her ongoing role of mother and sister and friend to me. She and Melvin had years before taken on responsibilities as pseudo grandparents. Our children happily had accepted that and clutch them even now so tightly in their arms and hearts.

The next morning, I called my mother and stepfather on the phone in Florida to tell them that John was gone. I mentioned the plan for his service, and they told me that they would not attend. They still traveled to the Caribbean and Europe, but felt no urge, no responsibility to come to us. I somehow was still surprised by the news. Ironically, my mother had often said to me, "Never expect a good change of behavior from someone who has disappointed you." Likely meant as a slight to my father, she was that very person she decried, and I had foolishly continued to hope for more.

My sister wanted to come, but by then, I knew better than to encourage that.

I did not feel alone. I embraced and accepted the kindness that my surrogate mother, Sheila, and my family of friends offered. I got through the tough times to come, sometimes with their help, and sometimes on my own.

I did worry about the effects of this tragedy on my seventeen and fifteen year old children. Could I still manage to be a better mother than was my own? I had always been so driven to do that. Had I neglected them while I nursed their father?

I had so little fathering. I had counted on my husband to be that giant among men, a wise patriarch who would counsel them well. Would Caroline or Ivan remember any of what their father had said or taught them? After all, John had been sort of absent for the four years of his illness. I mourned my husband's absence and was grief-stricken at our little family's loss of structure. Somehow we hung on.

Five years later, I married a kind and thoughtful man who has created his own good relationships with both Caroline and Ivan. I am always hopeful that they remember some of the good character of their father. And that they continue to learn from Paul.

I worry still and feel inept often. Did I get the job done right? Did I raise my children better? Did I teach them well?

Just when such thoughts overwhelm me, I see Caroline setting her table with linen and flowers. Or Ivan calls to discuss the percentage of income one should give to charity. They are polite and well spoken. They look in the eyes of the person to whom they are introduced and give a firm handshake. They are both generous and kind.

And in those moments, I realize that no one taught me to do those things. My mother and father didn't. My sister Laurie does not model these behaviors. I simply watched Enid and Doris and then Sheila. And I made a conscious choice to be like them, to be parented by them, to parent like them. To take what I observed, and then do all I could to get it right.

Like the lone survivor in the science fiction movie, I did what I had to do. I created a new world of my own. Yes, my planet blew up. But by digging through the ashes and debris, I found the needed material to be the mother and to build the family I never had.

LOCATION, LOCATION, LOCATION

LOCATION, LOCATION, LOCATION

DIANNE ELLIOTT

IN MY LIFE, I COUNT many elders who helped me stay on the right path, steered me back on to it, or led me to it. However, one always stood out as the first one. That would be my next-door neighbor, Louise Malm Fisher: a diminutive in stature, but commanding in presence, first generation Swedish-American and lifelong friend of my grandmother and mother. She personified the significant "elder," who made all the difference in the quality of the life I sought and lived.

Her entrance into my life began before my emergence into the world. She drove my mother to the hospital for my birth. She squeezed her one-year and seven-year-old sons into the car, along with my mother and grandmother for the eight-mile drive to the hospital where I would be born. She told me that story many times, so proud that she had a literal part of my entrance into this world.

Because her younger son Dan was only a year older than I, she often said that we were almost twins and our names, Dan and Dianne, phonetically sounded as though we were. Many times, she told me I embodied the daughter she never had, which thrilled me to the moon and back. I became a fixture at their house next door, and a frequent part of their family outings. Their family portrait filled in the cracks of my personal foundation, so very imprecise in my birth home.

Part of her family representation included "normal" activities that occurred on a predictable basis: watching Ed Sullivan on Sunday nights or playing Scrabble or Monopoly every Saturday, always followed by toast and Louise's homemade applesauce, or going to "Nick's," a dive of a joint, eight miles away, for hamburgers on Fridays, even in a snowstorm.

Her positive 'can do' attitude on life filled that lack of incentive persistent in my home. She insisted on photographing milestones in my life, such as my confirmation in the Episcopal Church, with their living room as the background. This served, once again, to reinforce her literal presence in my life's landmarks. She often told me how proud she was of my straight A's in my studies and how I tackled learning to play the clarinet, even though my ear-splitting practices must have been excruciating for her to endure, even a house away.

Then, a memory lingers of Dan with me on the makeshift backseat, preparing to launch his homemade hotrod on the three-block downhill journey to summer camp. This ill-fated inauguration quickly ended after he miscalculated the first turn, pitching the two of us into a ditch. Dan, unhurt, continued on foot to the camp.

Louise scooped me up, scraped and shaken, back to her house where she pampered me with toast and orange juice as she ministered to my scratches and bruises. I felt safe and sheltered by her in her home, after this scary experience. Ironically, I do not remember my mother or grandmother's presence at all during this incident.

She asked me to baby-sit her infant granddaughter, entrusting me to take her on an excursion for a number of blocks from their house to her son's new home. I remember feeling so proud and responsible that she thought me so capable and dependable.

Louise's positive presence in my early life cemented the pivotal alignment upon which my future paths depended. Without her quiet and powerful message that I was worthy of love and that I was gifted to do anything I set my mind to do, I fear that my life could have been circumscribed by that small town, ingrained with its lack of ambition and direction like so many who were born there. She gave me the same loving direction that she gave her two sons: "do not settle for less than the best you can do."

Education became her paramount message for escaping the shortsighted confines of that rural setting. She would often remark, "The time will pass anyway so why not have achieved something worthwhile at the end?" I remember that missive as I found my way to escaping the town for nursing school in a large city and as I continued my journey to further educational ventures. She was always there, figuratively, on my shoulder, with her words of encouragement and her belief in my capabilities to be whomever I chose to be. Implicit in her message, which affected my actions, emerged a core appreciation that I was worthy of love and deserved to be valued.

My fate, in a life filled with challenges, heartbreaks, disappointments and subsequent triumphs over those hurdles, depended on one woman who lived next door, and that made all the difference.

ONE IN A MILLION

Dianne Elliott

As a student at my small high school in central Pennsylvania, I had two options of study: college prep or technical. Luckily for me, I chose the former. That decision put me in the company of G. Lane Rosensteel, my English teacher for three years and Latin teacher for two. His influence sanctioned me to choose the right fork in the path to a worthwhile life.

Those of us in the college prep also participated in the high school band, debating club and, in general, displayed traits of ambition to escape the hellhole that was our small town.

Mr. Rosensteel, or "Lane," as we sometimes irreverently called him, was a cool dude. His clothes conveyed a sense of preppie with a European flair and we later learned, his shoes came straight from the mills of Italy. His demeanor reflected a casual, unruffled calm that bedeviled us to try and infiltrate. A refined, almost feminine, aura surrounded him. Although we found that noteworthy in our town of *macho-ness*, we quickly dismissed inquiry or chatter about these traits when he mentioned a girlfriend. We thought him too even tempered to be "odd."

As a teacher, he displayed a sense of dramatic humor and sophistication about life in general that we found intriguing. For example, he watched only foreign films and often rhapsodized about the earthy beauty of Sophia Loren, of whom we barely had recognition.

This histrionic stamp became enhanced when he showed his passion for the Latin language, as he explained its primary foundation in our English linguistic origins. His voice developed animation as he gave myriad examples of the ancestries for everyday words that emanated from their Latin roots. At the time, our class summarily dismissed this passion as his alone. Years later I sheepishly appreciated this elemental truth, as I tried to translate a word in Italian or Spanish, when I traveled abroad.

We often tried to crack his aplomb, about the beauty of all things Latin, by jokingly translating our homework in a literal manner. For example: instead of Lavinia's hair catching fire we would surreptitiously agree to translate it as "Flames occupied the hair of Lavinia." He would, good-naturedly, roll his eyes and move on with the passage.

Another device, we utilized to break the spell of his reverie about the Latin language, involved one of us rattling our lunch bag or papers loud enough to be a distraction. Again, he would sigh and continue with his discussion.

In our English classes, his intense emotion about language, and its beautiful uses, continued as he noted a paragraph of outstanding writing from a former student's assignment or from a newspaper article he'd saved. This enthusiasm filtered down to us even though we resisted its import with humor or attempted to minimize its significance in our readings.

Gradually, under his influence, and much to our chagrin, our excitement about reading great works of literature, with appreciation, seemed less foreign to ourselves.

Personally, I always loved language and literature; this became my escape route from a home life that wanted for normalcy. I welcomed the assignments and took my literature books home even when I did not have a required reading. In fact, I had to feign ignorance about why I carried my literature book home on a weekend, when it was noted by my friends. I would reply, "Oh, I didn't even notice I had it with me."

Lane required essay writing on various subjects, and he gave detailed feedback on each paper. I eagerly anticipated reading his comments and I swear that I beamed at his positive notes and subconsciously incorporated his suggestions for improvement into my fund of knowledge for future writing.

The subject on our final essay, in our senior year, focused on why we chose our post-high school field of study. Since I planned to attend nursing school, I wrote of that intent. His remarks figured to be prescient as he noted, "This is your weakest essay; your heart doesn't seem to be in your writing here." I never forgot that line as I later, emotionally, struggled with becoming a nurse.

in the middle year of my three-year nursing program, I felt increasingly, desperately unhappy and unfulfilled. Outside my student nursing life, I cultivated a circle of friends from Carnegie Mellon University (CMU) who were dramatics majors, or "dramats" as they named themselves. I savored my time in their presence where their creativity flourished, and their mode of dress mirrored their bohemian leanings. I wanted to live that life, not just be a follower.

I decided that I would write to Lane, explain my situation, and ask his opinion if he thought I had the intellect and background to apply to CMU.

Lane immediately wrote back and cautioned me not to make a rash decision when I seemed so conflicted. He reassured me that he had no doubts that I would be accepted and succeed at CMU. He advised that since I was halfway through the nursing program, I consider finishing. Not only would completing the program give me a sense of accomplishment but it would also provide a means of skilled employment while I considered other opportunities. He ended the letter by including his personal phone number and the invitation to call him anytime if I felt the need to talk.

I finished the program and he came to my graduation. I will never forget his professional and personal availability to me in that time of crisis.

Just as he instilled a love of reading, writing, and language by his teaching, he proved his compassion and availability to a young woman who, at that time, had very few mentors in her life. That presence forever embedded itself in my grateful memory by his example of selfless actions and passion for his work.

I carried those examples forward into my life as I found my own fervor and pathway to authenticity.

ROMA BELLA/ IL GATI DI ROMA

Dianne Elliott

G ANDHI SAID, "THE GREATNESS OF a nation shall be judged on how its animals are treated." The Italians, and particularly the Romans, exemplify the consummate depiction of that statement.

Roma, the Eternal City, is like no other place in my experience. Besides the daunting array of history, architecture, culture and culinary opportunities the City offers for exploration, another lifestyle characteristic emerges: the Roman's love and respect for animals.

The Area Sacra, where ancient ruins poke from the earth in the middle of the City, houses a cat sanctuary. Felines, of all colors and sizes, roam, sleep, and live amid these remains. Their coats look thick and shiny. Their demeanor, languorous and indolent, speaks to their sense of security as they reside in the center of the bustling and a noisy Roman reality, the Avenue Vittorio Emmanuelle, just a city block away. This habitude, founded by two Roman women, subsists solely on monetary, bedding, and food donations from locals and tourists. A serene co-existence of sacred antiquity and less fortunate living beings stages a vibrant tableau of Roman empathy.

Repeatedly in diverse sections of the City, I viewed the reverence with which Romans respected their animals-whether pets or strays. Dogs dined with their owners in outdoor cafes; cats slept peacefully at the entrance to

47

their homes amid the cacophony of Roman traffic. People put bowls of food and milk by their doors for strays, and both cats and dogs sat on the laps of their owners on countless benches and parks throughout the City.

One particular incident branded this attribute in my memory. On one afternoon as siesta approached and rain started to fall, I concluded my visit to Il Foro. As I proceeded to leave the site, I witnessed an unforeseen indelible *scene*.

Approaching Il Foro, via the dirt-covered road, put-putted a three–wheeled, Italian mini car stirring up dirt and spitting stones from its pathway. While the car slowly coughed and chugged up the hill, cats started to appear from seemingly nowhere. One, then three, then ten, until finally I guessed thirty, magically emerged as if some whistle blew, that only they could hear.

Visually, their physical differences provided striking contrasts. There were skinny –ribbed mamas with their litter hanging on to them–sometimes literally. Ratty-eared toms strutted confidently in the lead and their body language suggested a cautious awareness of their surroundings. Others in various stages of malnutrition displayed a more skittish manner as they emerged from the clay and dirt scrub, as if their hierarchy in the group was not in the Alpha tier. The modus operandi of the pack rendered a vigilance borne from survival of the fittest. The closer they moved toward the car, the less tentative their demeanor, as if they had played this scene before and knew the conclusion *to be favorable.*

Ever so patiently, they waited as the old woman behind the wheel slowly got out of the car; she wore a faded and threadbare dress suggesting she came from a very modest social class. She moved with a painful and careful certainty as she cracked the passenger door and perched an umbrella between the door and the roof of the car to shield the rain. With exquisite attention, she placed ten or so paper plates beside the car, onto which she heaped spaghetti and meatballs from a large pot. The cats sat quietly, and some would say politely, until she stepped back and motioned them to partake of the fixings.

They converged upon the meals as if pulled by some magnetic force. As they ate, growling sounds of hunger mixed with purrs as they rowdily gulped their meal. The rain gently tapped on the umbrella shielding them, as if in tune with their pleasure.

After the cats polished off their meals, she gathered the plates, placed them onto the front seat, folded the umbrella and sputtered off in her tiny triangular vehicle. The satiated felines dissolved into the terrain of Il Foro, as if what I had just experienced had been a mirage.

I stood there spellbound by this simple, yet profound, act by an old woman of simple means sharing her food with these seemingly feral animals. This emerged as another example of Romans revering all living beings, no matter their place in the hierarchy of civilization.

Upon returning to the US, this memory became a cue and call to action. So, moved by this altruistic coda by which the Romans lived to the fullest, I was inspired to volunteer at animal shelters and advocate for the ethical treatment of all living beings. To this day, it remains an essential part of my lifestyle.

SICILIA: CUORE MIA

Dianne Elliott

YOU DON'T MAKE IT EASY. After years of pining for you, I am finally getting the chance to meet you. Then, our meeting gets canceled at the last minute and cannot be re-scheduled for days. I am heartbroken and in shock. How could you be so insensitive to my yearning?

Here I stand, at Logan Airport, in Boston, eager to board the flight to Rome, which will connect me to the flight to Palermo and two glorious weeks in Sicily. But wait; nothing is happening after all the fuss in getting the Premium Economy and us regular old Economy passengers lined up for this long-awaited trip. Tension becomes palpable as some intuitive sense of foreboding permeates the room. Murmurs crescendo into exclamations of concern as the time for departure comes and goes. Rumblings of discontent mingle with exasperated sighs as the Alitalia staff keep their heads glued to computers and avoid any direct eye contact.

Finally, an impatient passenger strides up to the boarding desk, gestures excitedly and turns back to the restless crowd with arms extended shouting, "The flight is canceled!" Murmurs of disbelief turn to a humming swell of outrage, as, at last, the Alitalia desk supervisor confirms that, indeed, the flight is canceled "due to technical issues."

This bad news is further heightened by the second announcement that all flights are completely booked for days, but they will try to get us on some partner airlines. The mayhem begins as the crowd's behavior ranges from outrage to tears to stunned disbelief at the sorry reality of a disrupted vacation emerges. People walk in aimless circles and clutch their cells phones as they convey their misfortune to loved ones.

By now, it is after 11PM and I elect to leave the airport, stay with a friend in Boston, and deal with this sorry mess tomorrow. I retrieve my luggage, find a cab and stumble into a friend's condo in Back Bay, which takes another ninety minutes.

The next morning, my anxiety starts to surface. My friend is already in Rome and on her way to Palermo. I frantically try to inform her of this disaster. The next wake-up call: the next flight I can book is three days away and no," there is no alternative," my travel agent informs me, "sorry."

The good news is I can stay with longtime friends and have unexpected reunions. So that I do.

Even though there is a Nor'easter on the day I finally leave, the flight takes off on time and, with nary a bump, we climb to our cruising altitude. My connection in Rome goes without a hitch. I finally set foot on Sicilia terra firma!

We rent a car and I elect to drive, as our trip to Trapani, on the way to Erice, is only one and a half hours. Driving on the Autostrada seems surprisingly stress-less, that is, until we come to an abrupt halt after thirty minutes. Stopped traffic stretches as far as I can see. And, in typical Italian fashion, people have left their cars and stand chatting and smoking along the road, resigned to make the best of the situation. Finally, I learn from some American military personnel, stranded nearby, that a tractor trailer has jack-knifed and spilled gasoline over the road.

After many police cars and ambulances screech by, the fire department finally arrives on scene to begin the clean-up. Two hours pass before we are on our way to Trapani, once again.

Now it is beginning to get dark and we need to find the parking lot near the Port of Trapani where we can park our car and take the Gondola up to Erice, the medieval city perched on the top of a nearby mountain. Trapani, alive with Saturday night revelry, becomes an endless, confusing maze. Locals give us multiple different directions to the Port parking structure, as they try to be helpful, unable to translate our fractured Italian queries.

After two hours of this frustration and endless circling the same streets, I announce to my friend that we need to drive up to Erice as the last Gondola of the night has departed.

So up to Erice we go: seven miles of a barely two-lane road with repetitive hair pin turns, as the lights of Trapani become tiny dots below. Being fearful of heights makes me focus only on the road in front of me and at last we come to Erice, which appears out of the fog like a miracle.

Since my travel delay has re-arranged our itinerary, we have only one night in Erice. Consequently, I have to re-live my drive down the mountain the next day- in the horror of daylight and comprehension of how steep the plunge to our death will be if I miscalculate a turn.

Agrigento, our next stop, awaits us and entails a three-and-a-half-hour drive, (even though Rick Sleeves swears that no destination in Sicily is farther than three hours). Our route quickly exits the Autostrada for secondary roads and roundabouts, where the Italians soundly demonstrate that rules of roundabouts are unknown to them. I abruptly recall that my days as a Boston driver barely prepares me for survival here. However, I persist as my hands cramp from clutching the steering wheel for dear life and my neck and head muscles morph into a tortuous mass of tension.

Still, amid this stress, I cannot fail to marvel at the majesty of this part of Italy. Mountains jut up in regal coupling and ruins of medieval temples are an unexpected, but common sight, perched among them. The topography seemingly changes with each segment of the trip, causing involuntary "awes" to emerge from me as though I were a child experiencing my first magical sight of mountains, or verdant valleys, or sights of the ocean.

Finally, we arrive at our destination in the Old Quarter of Agrigento. We then discover that there is no "there, there" as our street address doesn't seem to exist, even as the GPS, in a bedeviling auto voice announces, "you have arrived." Again, our trial and error attempts to communicate in third rate Italian produce confused stares and shoulder shrugs as to this address. Finally, an old man understands and directs us up a flight of stairs where our Vicolo hides behind the main thoroughfare! The door is locked, and the doorbell hangs by a frayed cord. Exhausted and desperately needing a WC, we sit on the stairs trying to contemplate what our next move should be. After what seems like an hour, the door opens and our host steps out to welcome us as if there is nothing unusual about us sitting on the steps with our luggage.

This occurrence presaged our future in navigating Sicilian roads and finding our lodging: we spend an hour trying to find our address is Pozallo; we drive in circles in Syracusa and finally lose the battle of attempting to successfully navigate the tiny, tortuous streets with our oversized Volvo (one damaged headlight and fender seriously marred trying to turn at a right angle in a Vicolo). Luckily, we don't know these future challenges at this time, early in the trip, so we blunder on blinded by the incredible magnetism of this place.

Instead, currently charmed by our host and the lovely abode, we quickly fall in love with, yet another aspect of this breathtaking and entrancing region, named Sicilia. All stress is forgotten, and any misadventures forgiven, as its enchanted presence takes hold once again.

ROOM FOR ALL

DIANNE ELLIOTT

HOUTZDALE, PENNSYLVANIA, A COLLECTION OF 1200 beleaguered souls and a few desolate stores, is located twenty miles east of Penn State University and one hundred twenty miles east of Pittsburgh. Green hills once surrounded the town, before the strip-mining companies ravaged them, and left the remains to fester, like an angry wound. Their blackened crevices became a visual curse of living in central Pennsylvania. This destitute place, in which I grew up, and from which I desperately sought to escape, constructed my earliest memories of emotional and cultural wanting.

My grandmother lived in Houtzdale her entire life. She refused to join my grandfather in Washington, D.C. when his promotion to Colonel in the U.S. Army assigned him to the Pentagon. They eventually divorced because she stubbornly refusal to abandon Houtzdale. My mother had left and then returned after her first marriage imploded. My grandmother continued her lifetime role of rescuer to her only child. I had a deep fear that I would become as destitute of spirit and self as they were if I stayed in this town. I needed to get out and never return.

In high school I emerged as an A student, member of the band and chorus and followed the college preparatory path of study. These choices acquainted me with others: those who also wanted to escape the cultural wasteland of our locale. We knew we could do better than the myopic inhabitants, lacking skill or education, left behind to slowly implode in that sham of a town.

My first escape plan: nursing school in Pittsburgh. I wanted to get out of that central area of Pennsylvania. For me it seemed like the remains of a skeleton, picked clean and left to deteriorate.

During my three years in the nursing program, I rarely returned to my birthplace. Pittsburgh offered me the cultural and sensory opportunities that I craved.

After graduating with an RN, still feeling a need for further intellectual inspiration, I left Pittsburgh for the cultural mecca of Boston and New England. I looked forward to new relationships imprinted with the sophistication of Boston's ambiance.

Fast-forward thirty-five years: I achieved my educational goals, lived in many exciting cities, and traveled to far-off countries.

Imagine my surprise when I answered my office phone in Seattle and heard a male voice who identified himself as one of one of my high school classmates. Shocked that he had tracked me down (he boasted he was a former detective), I reeled when he invited me to our high school reunion at a classmate's hunting camp. I stammered and struggled to find a way to politely decline. He said everyone was "curious" to know about my life since departing Houtzdale: where had I lived; was I married; did I have children?

Once again, I felt *different*. I had escaped from Houtzdale. Why did they want me to return? He brought me up to date on the lives of the other attendees. Most had predictable (marriage, children, widowed, divorced) histories and some, even though they ventured as far as a few hundred miles away, returned to the security and predictability of the place where they grew up. The prospect of spending time and money to return to the source of my worst nightmares left me with no rational reason to accept the invitation.

However, as I pondered this unexpected request, I could not help but feel touched by the outreach to me. I had smugly abandoned them for a life that I deemed richer in every way, but they kindly included me and sought my return to reconnect.

Consequently, a niggling thought crept into my consciousness. Was I afraid that a revisit to my old homestead would raise an error in my certainty about my life choices? Did those who remained, or returned, there mark their choices as positive instead of a failure to contemplate another option? Did their satisfaction with a simple lifestyle suggest that they, like Thoreau, could simply travel widely in spirit from that small town they called home? Did their fulfillment with needing familiar surroundings and quiet lives challenge my essential quest to purge that period of my history?

I did not attend the reunion. The process of how I arrived at that decision provided me with a new sense of harmony with those who lived, and stayed, in the same locale for all, or most, of their lives. Although I selected a life diametrically opposed to theirs, I found a different respect for their intrinsic choices. With these thoughts came a realization, that I could peacefully co-exist with the recognition, that our choices included us all in the fabric of humanity.

THE WORD AND I

DIANNE ELLIOTT

FROM MY EARLIEST MEMORIES, I loved to read, and the words of the stories always captivated my attention. Why did this word strike such a chord? Where did this phrase originate? How did using this particular word make the sentence come alive? When I engaged with words, they took me on a magical journey far from the present reality of a circumscribed and often unpleasant time. That trajectory enveloped me in a safety cocoon; it also set my course on a path where learning by reading became a cloak of love that sheltered me emotionally and fed my soul.

From this love of language, becoming an English teacher seemed like a natural segue. However, in the small-minded sphere of my high school guidance counselor, that choice marked a foolhardy path. Becoming a nurse or a teacher was much more practical as a prelude to marriage and motherhood. Therefore, I deferred my dream for the reality prescribed for small town girls at that time and place. The love for words never died although it remained a subconscious resolve that someday I would fulfill my dream to get a degree in English.

My personal life took twists and turns, and my professional identity did not support my ubiquitous yearnings for reading poetry or literature. World travels left me wanting for more than just the memories and different roles in nursing only paved another pathway to the same career dissatisfaction. Disquiet filled my life with the feelings of being off course in my journey to a more challenging and genuine intellectual reality.

My lack of having a bachelor's degree limited my options in advancing my nursing career. That comprehension also provided awareness that I could pursue my undergraduate degree as a double major in Nursing and English. I did not pursue the English degree as a formal goal but assiduously plotted a pathway where I would take all the required classes for that major while completing my bachelor's degree in nursing.

This duality proved more challenging than I ever presumed. However, the pursuit of my long slumbering dream to become an English major fueled my intent to succeed this time. This goal also extended my time at Boston College by two semesters. My final semester consisted of four English courses on my docket: Shakespeare; Linguistics; Literary Criticism and The Transcendentalists in American Literature.

That workload proved almost insurmountable in the time it demanded for the reading and writing assignments.

More than one Friday evening found me reading required coursework as my friends came by to pick me up for a weekend party. Their incredulous comments about my dedication and bookworm inclinations provided them with continued amusement. However, I ignored their teasing as I continued my ardent immersion into the world of words.

At the successful completion of that semester, (with A's in every subject) the formalities of declaring myself a double major in Nursing and English remained the final step.

The Dean of the Nursing School told me that the caseload was too heavy, and she could not approve it. With smug satisfaction, I informed her that the coursework was completed and to please sign on the line. The Dean of the English Department exclaimed that the department prohibited taking four English courses in one semester due to the disproportionate demands it placed on a student. He then expressed astonishment that this detail had slipped by the registrar. Once again, I asked for his signature and went on my way.

Accomplishing that milestone remains the pinnacle of my life's achievements by attaining a goal that eluded me for so many years.

My pride in the attainment of fulfilling my English degree still gives me chills when I realize I actually crossed that finish line.

MISFORTUNE AND HARDLY FAME

Dianne Elliott

I WAS RECRUITED TO A JOB at a prestigious Boston teaching hospital as the Director for Perioperative Services, doubling the salary I currently made at the small hospital north of the city. My present role continued to be eroded due to budget constraints, so it did not take a soothsayer to predict its imminent demise.

Who could refuse such a fabulous opportunity for a more noted title, high-class colleagues and the stimulating atmosphere of working in Boston every day? I could not and I did not, and the pathway away from my heart's work found its first paving stone.

First adjustment: instead of driving ten minutes to work, I now drove sixty to ninety minutes in hair-raising traffic and frequently hideous weather. This became necessary in order to arrive at this hospital's unofficial, but strongly subscribed, starting time of 7 A.M. To meet the deadline, required me rising at 4:40, A.M. and being on the road by 5:30 A.M. in order to avoid the back up of traffic on the Tobin bridge, one of the northern portals into Boston. I needed to arrive at my office preferably twenty minutes prior to 7 in the morning to psychologically gird myself for the demands of the ten to twelve-hour day ahead, with its omnipresent stress and conflict.

The next four years were filled with challenging expectations and resonating failures every step of the way. Among the more significant was developing and mentoring managers, including weeding out the dead wood among the crop I inherited, and also retraining veteran staff to improve their productivity in delivering patient care. These tasks proved to be daunting to me in mind, effort, and outcomes. They would serve as a major symbol of disappointment and frustration in my memory of this role.

The nursing department was recognized for its innovative development of the case management model, improved quality and effectiveness in patient care delivery. Requests for training other nursing staff from all over the state. All upper-level managers were strongly encouraged to author and deliver professional development lectures within their area of expertise to meet these needs. Another administrative expectation required this group to conduct seminars for the local and statewide professional organizations and become a board or committee member. What began as challenging became overwhelming, when tacked onto a twelve-hour workday topped by a two-hour commute. That became the crazy reality of my life working in the Big City. This frenetic pace compromised my sanity and buried my real sense of identity beneath this chaos and bureaucracy.

I became more and more frustrated at managing others instead of working independently and being solely accountable for my actions. I also became progressively unable to ignore the collective callousness and gallows humor that presented itself all-too-frequently in the burned -out caregivers in healthcare. My mental fatigue and physical exhaustion left me increasingly overwhelmed. I gave up trying to address these issues.

My increased income only caused me to buy myself more things, which I rationalized as my reward for surviving the stress of the job and the hellacious commute. However, these purchases, driven by the anxiety of my life, never filled "the hole" that seemed to open up in my soul. My life's work continued to move adrift from my moral compass. I felt unmoored. These thoughts floated in and out of my consciousness during my daily commute, and early one morning those reflections rushed catastrophically into my reality.

While driving through a downtown Boston intersection at 6AM, (returning back to work after less than ten hours away), a hit-and-run driver struck my car broadside, pushed it into a lamppost, which caused the car to roll onto its roof. Suspended upside down by my seatbelt with the Eurhythmics still singing, I half-consciously wondered if this was *The End*. It was not. My car was totaled but I miraculously escaped with only a concussion, a few bruises and many flashbacks for months to come when driving through intersections.

That wake-up call, which made clear my insane professional lifestyle and commute and coincided with another kind of call. It was from a recruiter asking if I was interested in a position available at a health sciences center in Portland, Oregon. Why shouldn't I explore this unexpected opportunity, I asked myself. At the least, it offered a free trip to Oregon, a state that had captured my love on a road trip years before.

Three months later found me stepping off of a plane in Portland and starting a new chapter in the same book, but in a different location. However, the unchanged existential issues that plagued me in my role in Boston would follow me here.

Commuting, thankfully, telescoped from two hours on an interstate to twenty minutes on a two-lane road. Another unexpected benefit in this new job: being appointed to the University Art Committee by my boss, the CEO of the Medical Center Hospital. This, unwittingly, began my love affair with Northwest Contemporary Art, as an art committee member and a beginning collector. The immersion in both undertakings awakened a passion in me that surpassed the steadfast disengagement I still found in my administrative role. This involvement in the arts changed my life, in momentous ways, unrevealed to me at the time, but that is another story.

Fast forward to another four years of living with disturbingly similar administrative frustrations. This disenchantment was barely kept at bay by my extensive involvement in the arts community. Helping to recruit a boss who progressively demonstrated a mental problem cunningly disguised as brilliance, propelled me to look for a professional exit.

Good-bye Portland and welcome to Seattle. Again, a recruiter enticed me to a position at the largest hospital in the northwest. My salary had doubled from my job in Oregon, plus I had an opportunity to live in a larger, more diverse city and work in a new professional setting. My first request was, not for my huge corner office, but to become an art committee member of the first and largest hospital collection in the northwest. My administrative skill quickly got me promoted to overseeing the art budgets for the new construction projects, which were part of the hospital's rapid expansion plan.

Though they were not part of my official role, I became truly engaged in these fulfilling assignments in the art projects. As my passion for art increased, I set sail on a course, unknown to me at the time. However, as my soul's compass soon pointed me in this new direction, I knew my corporate days were numbered.

FROM HITHER TO YON

HOW TO BECOME AN ANXIETY SPONGE

Irene M Hubbard

M Y MOTHER WAS THE PERSON who had the most influence on me in my formative years and into adulthood. My sisters were much older, so I was more like an only child.

One of the defining events in mother's life was a post-partum depression, which occurred after my birth, and lasted many years. After that experience, she was determined to never get depressed again. Her plan for that was to stay busy.

She was a courageous woman who built a summer house with my father on weekends, as if that is what all wives did. She packed us up every weekend for years and years, traveling back and forth between home in Mt. Vernon and Rocky Point Long Island when the only road was Route 25A, long before the Long Island Expressway was built. She had to cook outside on an open fireplace initially, and we all used an outhouse until we dug the cesspool and completed the bathroom.

I grew up feeling protective toward my mother. I think I knew on a molecular level, or at least subconsciously, that there was an emotional fragility about my mother, and I tried to lower anxiety around her.

When I was a senior in high school, I was working twenty-nine hours a week in a supermarket. My mother wanted to take a sewing class at night. She wouldn't go alone, so I took the class with her, and not because I didn't have enough demands on my time. The fact that I hated sewing didn't enter my mind.

One thing that worried my mother was my father's heart. The chiropractor had told my father that he had a bum ticker. My mother was afraid that all the physical labor of building the summer house would cause a heart attack. She told me to work by his side to lighten his load.

When I was nineteen years old and had been working at the phone company for a full year and was eligible for vacation time, my parents and I drove out to Long Island to our summer house for a weekend. My father and I walked down the gully and found that the drain we had built out of concrete had been blown apart. The house sat on the side of a sand cliff overlooking the Long Island Sound. The drain was meant to prevent the gully from eroding deeper and taking our house. Initially my father hadn't built a dry well at the street, so the rainwater runoff carried sand and deposited it at the bottom of the drain causing a blockage. The water pressure blew the top off the drain and dug a channel beneath it causing it to collapse.

I knew where I was going to be spending my vacation when I saw the look of defeat on my father's face. I lied and told my parents that the phone company would only let me take one week at that time. I actually was entitled to two weeks, but I was merely an over-responsible daughter, not a masochist.

I grew new muscles that week swinging a pickaxe, because I wasn't strong enough to heave the sledgehammer. My dad and I busted up the old concrete, cursing the fact that we had reinforced it with old pipes and wire lathe, and shoveled in sand where it had washed away.

We built new frames and filled them with concrete to repair the drain. To an uninformed spectator it might appear that I was doing this to help my father. But I was actually doing it to keep my mother safe from anxiety and depression.

The main role I played in the family was that of a comic. I was the baby of the family so I could get away with pertinent comments without causing anger because nobody took me seriously. I would pull off some silly stunt or say something outrageously germane. That would jolt the mood, lessen anxiety, and enable family members to become more open.

My mother's quest, to keep busy to ward off depression, provoked her to run the volunteer lunch program at my elementary school, besides building a summer house on weekends. She also sewed, canned, baked, knitted, crocheted, re-finished and re-upholstered furniture, and caned and rushed chairs. She never did have time for another depression.

She did, however, lose her memory once from anxiety. It was when her oldest brother was dying of colon cancer, and she couldn't get any information out of his second wife. He lived in Florida and my mother still lived in New York. She was discussing it with my sister Janet, and got herself so worked up, that she decided to fly down and find out for herself what was going on. When my sister called my mother later to see if she had finalized flight plans, my mother asked, "What for?"

My sister said, "To go see your brother in Florida."

"Why would I want to do that?"

"Because he has cancer."

"He does? Does Dad know?" Mom said with shock in her voice.

They went back and forth like that for a while and then my mother asked, "Is anybody coming for Christmas?"

My sister told her that we were all coming and that my mother had already bought two legs of lamb for dinner. My mother reflected, "I wonder where I put them?"

When Janet called me to say that Mom had lost her memory, I commented that it was never too good in the first place. She then explained what had happened and I diagnosed it as a dissociative reaction from the anxiety of her brother being deathly ill. My mother had worked herself up into such a frenzy that she was going to fly in an airplane, something she had never done. And then she forgot everything.

Mom recovered her memory after talking to Dad and I didn't want to act overly concerned about her mental health, so I waited a day to call. However, when I reached her on the phone she said, "I wish you had called yesterday. I was going to say, 'Irene who?'"

When my mother was in her 90's, mildly senile, and in an assisted living facility, she managed to hide her memory problems behind a laugh. I remember when she was trying to convince her sister to move into the facility. She raved about the place pointing out its advantages and ended by saying, "And when you look out the window, you can see the water."

That prompted my aunt, with her arthritic hip, to swing her walker into action and amble over to the window to look outside. She turned to my mother and said, "Rose, it's a parking lot."

My mother laughed hysterically, as if the joke was on my aunt.

She handled senility with grace and humor and not the usual frustration and anger. My guess is that she no longer remembered being depressed or worried about a recurrence. But she did remember my sister Janet, who lived near her in Florida, until the day she died. She thought that I bore a striking resemblance to her daughter Irene.

FAMILY SECRETS

Irene M Hubbard

MY PARENTS OWNED THE TWO-FAMILY, stucco house in Mount Vernon, New York, where I lived from age five until I married. It was built on a hill and my mother constructed a flower garden down the length of the house, terracing it with rocks. The house didn't have outside space for playing. A clothes tree took up most of the back yard. I have a scar on my knee from that clothes tree. I banged into it just after having sutures removed from a gash in my knee and the wound dehisced, leaving a wide scar.

As a family of five, with three daughters, having only one bathroom was indeed problematic. The house also had only two bedrooms so my sisters, five and six years older than I, shared a bedroom with me that had one tiny closet, in the days of crinolines. My sisters occupied the far side of the bedroom, their beds separated by a large night table. They had all the windows on their side, and I was stuffed in a corner by the door, with a quilted fabric-covered, cardboard, bedside table that resembled a file cabinet, except that it was pink and made out of paper.

My sisters drew an imaginary line across the floor and told me that I could not cross into their space. They rigged their dresser drawers with pieces of string to provide a tell-tale signs should I ever open a drawer of theirs; something they probably learned from a Nancy Drew novel. I don't know why they treated me like the enemy because they were never forced to babysit for me. I was not a bother to them. They acted as if they had important stuff to hide but I had seen all their belongings and it held no interest for me.

Aside from the five of us, there were also pets in the house. The puppy my Dad brought home from work in his fedora (causing him to relinquish the use of that hat for a week, to keep the puppy from crying) turned out to be a small enough breed for our tight household, a Pomeranian mix.

We also had a mynah bird, whom my Dad taught to say, "Hi ya boy" in exactly the same pitch and tone of my father's voice. I think the bird had his wings clipped because I remember him hopping around on the kitchen floor terrorizing the dog.

Added to the menagerie were one parakeet, six tanks of tropical fish, and a tiger-striped alley cat called Skippy. The cat roamed the neighborhood all night and his face was scarred from cat fights. But, during the day he let me dress him in doll clothes and wheel him around in my doll carriage.

At one point my father was looking to buy a monkey, but Mom crushed that notion. Not to be outdone, she wanted to raise chinchillas, as a business. We convinced her that she'd never be able to kill them so within a short time the house would be overrun by luxuriant, velvety-skinned rodents.

We maxed out at five people, a cat, a dog, two birds, and dozens of fish living in about twelve hundred square feet. That's not counting the squirrels my father enticed into the sunroom with peanuts. Luckily, they would take the nuts and run.

My father was adept at creating space savers. The kitchen table was attached to the wall with metal brackets so there were no legs. He also made a desk in the kitchen and a desk chair that blended with the adjacent drawers and disappeared when tucked tightly under the desk.

Dad sat at that desk to take the phone order each afternoon. He was the produce buyer for a supermarket chain, Gristedes, and received the order in late afternoon for the fruit and vegetables he would buy that night at the produce market in lower Manhattan. He always worked nights, and we always had dinner at five o'clock so he could eat before leaving for work.

Sometimes, my father's call would occur while we were eating dinner. As he wrote down the amount to buy next to each item on his list he would say, "Yep," or "Right," My sisters and I would pretend to ask him questions.

"Can I have a dollar for nothing?" I would ask.

"Yep," My dad would answer, and my sisters and I would giggle.

"Am I the smartest in the family?" my sister Janet would ask.

"Right," my father would say and even my mother would stifle a laugh.

But, for the most part, there was very little talking at dinner, at least not in English. My parents learned Polish as their first language from their immigrant parents and they never taught it to my sisters or me. They were able to communicate secretly in plain sight. I think they planned it that way because there were so many family secrets.

One was a secret kept only from my sisters and me. We didn't learn about it until my father was dying. Before he was married, Dad had accidentally struck and killed a pedestrian while driving home from work one night in the dark. He never wanted his children to know. At his funeral while speaking with Aunt Nat about the closeness between my father and his brother John, she commented, "Yeah, he was driving John's car the night he hit that guy." And I had only found out about "that guy" three days earlier.

There were also breaches in my family that I knew nothing about. We lived in New York and the entire extended family was in Connecticut. We rarely saw them, so it was easy to hide a family cutoff. After the death of my father's parents, who died three months apart, my father remained connected with everyone, but none of the other four siblings ever spoke to Aunt Kate again for the rest of their lives.

Aunt Kate inherited my grandparent's house, but she had been living there for the last ten years taking care of my bedridden grandmother who had a fractured hip, and my senile grandfather.

I don't think it was the inheritance that alienated the siblings. Aunt Kate had control over access to their parents for many years. I believe the siblings felt that their sister Kate had restricted their time alone with their parents, especially their mother who still had all her faculties. Cutoffs in families often focus on money or inheritance, but they are usually triggered by age-old sibling rivalries around competition for a parent's attention.

When Aunt Kate died, she left her house to my sister Barbara.

I couldn't wait to call Barbara to say that I was contesting the will.

DANCING LIKE LOVERS

Irene M Hubbard

MY HUSBAND JACK AND I didn't dance when we were dating. We both liked dancing and prior to our relationship he had dated a ballerina. But Jack couldn't dance on time and I couldn't dance off time so together it was heart-rending.

I, too, had previously dated a good dancer who was not a professional himself but was taught by one, his former girlfriend. On Saturday nights in summer he and I went to the beach clubhouse dances and did the lindy, formerly known as the jitterbug and now called the swing. The crowd would gather round us to watch him throw me up in the air, and then between his legs. It was exciting.

For twenty years of marriage Jack and I avoided events where music and dancing would be part of the evening. I would experience a physical ache watching others dance and Jack would tap his feet off -time while we sat out the dances.

When the children were all off to various schools, and we were home alone for the first time since having children, we decided, almost simultaneously, to take dance lessons. There was a Fred Astaire dance studio in our town, so we signed up.

Jack spent the first class in a corner with his dance teacher for the entire hour. I was flying around the dance floor with the owner of the studio, as he expertly led me through the waltz, foxtrot, tango, cha cha, swing and rhumba. It was glorious. I was afraid that Jack was going to sour on the whole idea when I saw that he never moved from the corner.

On the way home Jack told me excitedly that he had learned some technique: posture, heel-toe placement on steps, and counting the rhythm, quick-quick-slow. He asked, "What did you learn?"

I said, "Nothing, I just danced." I was amazed that we were both equally enthusiastic for entirely different reasons and I knew in that moment that we were going to learn to dance together.

Well, we didn't just learn, we became addicted to ballroom dance. We converted our office on the third floor into a dance studio. We took out all the furniture, put in a hardwood floor padded with cork beneath, had floor to ceiling mirrors installed on one wall and installed a CD player for our strict tempo ballroom dance music. We were competitive dancers in no time because the studio pushed that as a money maker. We had to buy more lessons to compete.

I had to have a ball gown made and Jack's dance tuxedo was imported from England tailored to his measurements. No loose clothing on the men. Just as the women sprayed their hair into stiff agglomerations resembling cotton candy, the men's tuxedos didn't bulge or fold awkwardly. We acquired special dance shoes that had suede on the soles, and the women's heels had a rod of steel through the insole. Believe me, it was needed.

Although Jack was tone deaf, his teacher taught him how to dance by numbers. For instance, the cha- cha started with a rock step on the second beat. So, the count was two, three, four and one; or, rock step, cha cha- cha.

Jack was able to learn all the dances with the number technique except the tango. He was never sure when to begin that dance and I had to face away from the judges when we started the tango so they wouldn't see my lips saying, "Now."

Jack and I took two hours of dance lessons a week, one hour with our individual teachers and one hour as a couple. We got coaching from various former world champions who would come to Manhattan studios to coach professional and amateur couples. Once we got to the advanced levels in competition, we had choreographed dances. We shared our choreography with our dance instructors, who were a married couple. Four different couples danced the same choreography, the professional and the amateur couples and the two pro-am couples.

We also traveled to Maryland for coaching from a former national champion a couple of times a month. One of us would videotape each coaching session. We received coaching after a competition in Halifax, a half-way point for the reigning world champions who were from England.

I had to learn about makeup, as it was imperative to be visible to the judges when competing. I had never worn eyeliner or mascara before. I also had to cut my hair. I had hair long enough to put up in a twist, but then it would take a long time to wash out all the hair spray. After a competition the women with short hair would be ready to go out to dinner much faster than I.

When I took up dancing, my face changed, my hair changed, my posture changed, my style of dress changed, and my co-workers thought I was having an affair.

Jack, too, became more conscious of his appearance. While at a competition in Florida, the United States Ballroom

Championships, the designer of the women's gowns, took Jack clothes shopping at the vendor's booths. Although he was a conservative dresser, Jack came back with a glittery Latin dance jacket that he wore for many dances at the studio thereafter.

I had to have a spare bedroom for my ball gowns, because you can't hang them. They lived on a bed in the guest room. They were elastic on the top, covered with crystal stones, with flouncy skirts bordered by oodles of feathers. My last gown had epaulets which caused a problem going through doorways. One time I knocked a judge's clipboard right out of his hands with my epaulets as I swished by. I would do anything to get a judge to notice me.

Many mistakes are made during competitions. I remember losing my shoe during the Viennese Waltz while dancing with my teacher. I continued to dance with one shoe on and one shoe off, and my teacher didn't feel it. Afterwards when I went to retrieve my shoe from the judge he said, "Show off."

Another time my teacher ended up with the heel of another female dancer stuck in his shoe at the instep. He didn't feel it, but we noticed that wherever we went this pink dancer went with us. We dragged her down one wall before she finally got loose and spun off.

The last dance at the weekly studio parties was always a waltz, and Jack and I would dance it together. It was frequently the song, *Dancing Like Lovers*, by Ross Mitchell, Larry Herbstritt and Doug Thiele. I felt sad dancing that waltz because it meant the party was over. We could have danced all night, Jack and I.

It was astonishing to us how good we got together after the dance wasteland our marriage had been. It took perseverance, and we practiced every chance we got. We liked to go to the Roseland Ballroom in New York City, but sometimes it was dead. It's no fun dancing with a crowd that lacked enthusiasm. We danced at the Rainbow Room at Rockefeller Plaza in Manhattan once, which has a revolving circular dance floor in the center of the dining room. We frequently went down to SOB's in the Village, which is an abbreviation for Sounds of Brazil. We danced uptown at the Latin Club where we probably were the only non-immigrants in the room. We went to other dance studio parties that were open to the public all over New Jersey.

One night it was almost midnight when Jack got home from work and he wanted to go to the Latin Club. I was tired and asked why he would want to go out dancing at such a late hour. He said, "It is the anniversary of my father's death, and I am at the age he was when he died. I want to do something to feel alive."

"I'll get my shoes," I said.

We would buy strict tempo dance CDs at the competitions, and finally found one with our favorite waltz, "*Dancing Like Lovers*." That recording became very popular during our time of dancing and was played at many competitions. We used it to practice our choreographed waltz sequence. We carried the CD with us when we went away weekends. We practiced in places like the firehouse in Southport, Connecticut, a roller rink in Greenport, Long Island, and the basement of a church in Southold, Long Island.

After five years of dancing we were winning competitions. Once, at a Manhattan nightclub, the bandleader asked if we were pros. Our children would show our competition dance videotapes to their friends. We were dancing with no space between us from the waist down and splayed apart at the shoulders, like a champagne glass with a single stem. Jack learned to lead from the hips. He was easy to follow.

I stayed with the dance studio for a few months after Jack died. I could dance with other people and it was a diversion from grief. I went alone to dance parties all over the State. Grief can fuel an addiction and dancing was still mine. All I needed was one dance to demonstrate that I knew what I was doing, and my dance card would be filled for the night.

But, inevitably *"Dancing Like Lovers"* would start playing and I would abruptly leave.

BEST JOB EVER

Irene M Hubbard

IT WAS A PRIEST WHO showed me how to get into nursing school. I had been working at the phone company for two years. Although I loved that job and got all the overtime because I had learned all the positions and could tidy up the department on Saturdays, I really wanted to be a nurse. I just didn't know how to get there.

I had looked at a practical nursing school, which was a shorter program, but I didn't think they respected women. In their catalog they stated that students had to wear girdles, as if we were wanton women seducing patients. I was only twenty, but I recognized oppression. I had never worn a girdle in my life because they hurt.

One Friday night, when I was shopping in New Rochelle, New York, I went to confession in the parish across the street from Bloomingdales. The priest began to talk to me like a human being. It was post Vatican II, but I guess my parish hadn't caught up yet because I never had a priest ask me questions about my life. This one did and I told him about my job and that I wanted to become a nurse but didn't know how to do that, given that I had already wasted two years working. He asked me to meet him in the rectory. The priest gave me a catalog for Westchester Community College and told me about the two-year programs to earn a degree that would allow me to sit the exam to become a registered professional nurse.

I found a list of community colleges on the back of the catalog and applied to Bronx Community College because it was closer to my home. There was an entrance exam that I took on a Saturday. When I received a letter saying that I had been accepted into the program, I went to my father. Tuition was going to be $600 for the first year and I would need to use my Mom's car. He relented to both requests, so I went back to my high school job at the supermarket on Friday nights and Saturdays, to earn enough money for parking in the Bronx. I thought it would blow the whole deal if my father knew I had to pay to park.

Once I graduated from nursing school, I was so proud that I would travel to work with my nursing cap flung up on the dashboard in clear view. I wanted everyone to see I was a nurse. However, it didn't stop me from getting a traffic ticket in Pelham, New York.

I went on to complete my baccalaureate at Penn and my master's at NYU, and then I did post-graduate training in family therapy for four years at an institute in New Rochelle, where I eventually worked as a clinician. I also had a private practice in psychotherapy in New Jersey where I lived and was able to get third party reimbursement as a psychiatric clinical nurse specialist, a certification I obtained from the American Nurses Association.

When my husband disappeared off the face of the earth in an instant, he was brain dead after a fall, I didn't want to practice therapy anymore. I remembered how proud I had always been to be a nurse, and I thought it would be good to go back to hospital nursing which was less isolating. I called the Director of Nursing at Hackensack Hospital to see what she could offer, as she had been a classmate of mine at NYU. She didn't have anything at the time but called me a few months later to say that a position had opened up for a psychiatric clinical nurse specialist in a consultation liaison role.

I interviewed for the job and got it. My immediate supervisor had created the role in the hospital and we both had the same mission. I was to assist the nurses in caring for their patients throughout the hospital when there were issues of emotional health for the patient and/or the family. I dressed in a suit, carried a pager and worked afternoons and evenings when families were most likely to be visiting.

This was an amazing job for me. I got to use all my skills, even my ballroom dance expertise. One evening in the surgical intensive care unit I gave dance lessons to two nurses who were getting married and needed to learn the waltz. The following day my supervisor said to me, "I hear you were giving dance lessons in SICU?"

"Yes," I replied.

"Way to go." she said. Nurse morale was important to us.

The nurses paged me to see patients like the Garden State Parkway worker who had lost his leg, up to his buttocks, in a woodchipper. They often paged me to the cardiac step-down unit which was where patients were transferred three days after open heart surgery for cardiac bypass and graft surgery. They paged me to tell a medical student graduate from Sri Lanka that her husband had died in the same car accident which had put her into a coma for a few days with a closed head injury. And even family members could page me to see family members who were patients.

Once the nurses called me to see a patient who was calm and sane when I saw him, but had been outrageous the night before, pacing and ranting and raving in the hall and throwing chairs. After talking with the patient, I spoke with his doctor and told him that the patient needed a psych evaluation as he probably was bipolar, untreated. The doctor told me that he wasn't mentally ill, he was just agitated the night before because of a reaction to his meds.

I asked the doctor, "Did he tell you about the time he went shopping and bought seventy-five dress shirts?"

"No," the doctor said.

"Did he tell you about the time he got pulled over driving 125 mph on the thruway?"

"No," the doctor said.

How about the time he went seventy-two hours without sleep while hitting the slots at Atlantic City?"

I didn't know much about bipolar disorder except what I had studied in school, but I had done psychotherapy for eleven years, so I knew how to ask questions.

Another time a nurse called me to see a patient in the cardiac step-down unit whom she thought was depressed. He wasn't responding verbally, he refused to get up and walk to the bathroom, he wouldn't even turn his head and make eye contact.

I stood on the left side of the bed and addressed the patient. He ignored me. I walked around to the other side of the bed as he was facing that way and the patient did respond to my questions. He couldn't explain why he couldn't get up and use the bathroom, but it wasn't that he would not, it was that he felt he could not. I did not know what was going on with this man, except it wasn't depression. I asked the nurse to get a neurological evaluation, which she did.

The patient had experienced a stroke after his bypass surgery, which caused him to not recognize the left side of his body as his own. Later I read a book by the neurologist Oliver Sacks, who experienced the same sort of phenomenon, after a peripheral nerve injury which left him unable to claim his right leg as his own. He thought the medical students were playing a joke on him by putting a cadaver leg in the bed with him. Sacks experienced just as much difficulty explaining his disability as did my patient explaining why he couldn't walk, and Sacks was a neurologist.

I always read the complete chart before going in to see a patient. This was particularly important when I saw a patient in the cardiac step-down unit who was experiencing anxiety. He was hyper-vigilant, had insomnia and was shooting up his heart rate and blood pressure.

The patient told me about a dream he had in which the grim reaper came and stuffed him into a potato sack and started to drag him away, and then inexplicably released him. I asked the patient, "Did you know that your heart stopped during surgery and they had to resuscitate you?" He hadn't known but thought that it explained his dream, and his anxiety decreased greatly.

Then there was the little old lady with a frontal lobe benign tumor. I saw her post-operatively because she had asked to see me. She told me that her husband was physically abusive. I asked her if we could have her husband come in and talk about this with me. She agreed and her husband admitted that he had been hitting his wife. When I told the neurosurgeon, I knew what he was going to say.

"Have you met her husband? He's an 80-year-old man," he said, as if he never heard of elder abuse. He dismissed her words by saying, "She has swelling in her frontal lobe. You can't believe what she says."

I told him that I agreed, and that's why I had called in the husband, who confirmed the abuse. Referrals were made for appropriate care and follow up when she was discharged.

I left this job to go run a charter sailboat in the Caribbean with my son. I lost my certification by doing that, as I had to work continuously in the field to maintain it.

I think the real reason why I left was because I was afraid of being found out. I had not worked in a hospital for twenty-five years and I didn't know anything about nursing diagnosis, policy and administration. My boss and the nurses thought I was a superstar who would appear and work miracles, but I felt like a fraud. My only real education in nursing was at Bronx Community College because I advance placed out of the nursing courses at Penn and the degree at NYU was in the teaching of nursing, not practice. My nursing practice had been at a family therapy teaching institute, where most of my colleagues and students were social workers.

Even though I was good at what I did, I felt like I was out of my league embedded in a hospital nursing structure that was unfamiliar and had a lot of moving parts, called committees. Administration was an enigma.

So, I left the best job I ever had to work and live on a boat in the Caribbean with my youngest son who had just graduated from Massachusetts Maritime Academy.

NEW TO THE
CHARTER SAILBOAT BUSINESS

IRENE M HUBBARD

WHEN MY HUSBAND DIED, WE had a charter sailboat vacation scheduled, which I postponed for a few years. Finally, I invited a friend and her husband, and she invited her brother and his ex-girlfriend, because the current girlfriend's therapist said it was too early in the relationship for her to go on the trip, and two of my children invited a friend each, and we had a charter party.

We did a bareboat charter, which meant a charter without a captain or crew. I was certified as a captain at the Moorings, a charter boat business in the British Virgin Islands (BVI), where my husband and I had bareboat chartered several vacations. The boat is provisioned for most of the meals and has towels and linens onboard. They are very comfortable boats for groups to sail the BVI, where there is only a two-inch tide, no fog, and the trade winds blow at 15 knots or better. The coral reefs are visible in the clear water making them easy to avoid while sight-sailing from island to island. There is no need to plot a course or navigate.

That trip went off so well that it made me think that my son Christopher and I could run a sailboat charter business. Running some kind of a charter, or rental boat business was a common theme at the dinner table, when the kids were growing up, as a future family endeavor.

When Christopher graduated from Mass Maritime Academy, I asked him if he wanted to run a charter sailboat business with me in the Caribbean. He said yes and his brother went online and found us a boat. Chris and I went down to the Caribbean to see the boat and do a sea trial, and then I bought it without even bargaining. My financial advisor was against it, and rightfully so as it became a big money pit before it burned five years later, but it afforded so much fun for the family in the interim, that I never regretted it.

Christopher was taking US Coast Guard exams when I went down to the Caribbean to take possession of the sailboat, which had a captain and cook aboard. They left the next day after introducing me to the water maker, which they said I had to run every day or the membranes would become pickled, which sounded horribly painful. They also showed me the panel in the main saloon, which had dozens of switches and a couple of big, major switches. I was stunned by the sheer number and couldn't take in all the information but thought that I wouldn't be sailing the boat without Christopher and he probably knew what some of the words meant, like "inverter."

The crew left the next day and I began to open every compartment of the boat to take inventory. It was a pretty complicated beast with several air conditioners, each with their own fan and motor. An engine and generator sat below the floorboards along with many little containers, connected to hoses, through which water flowed, and which appeared to have clogged screens inside them. They were attached to tubing coming from the air conditioners. I decided they were filters and carried them to the deck to clean them.

While hosing down the first filter, my neighbors from the next boat yelled, "Watch out for the O ring," as I saw a black object fly into the drink.

"Where would one buy an O ring?" I asked the neighbors. Off to the chandlery I went, with my list and also my neighbor's list. I found out early that everyone helped each other in a charter community, and most didn't have a car. I had a rental car for the two weeks I was there to prepare for boat show.

Boat show was when the charter brokers came to the island and toured each charter boat meeting the captain and crew. They were there to generate our income by booking our boat for their clients. I wanted the boat to be spiffy. So, in addition to buying all new mattresses and pillows, comforters, linens and towels, I also hired someone to varnish the brightwork on the deck.

The comforters arrived in big boxes from Macy's in New Jersey, where I had purchased them, and were delivered to our clearing house, Flagship, where we got all our mail, and kept our charter calendar. Flagship had marine carts we could use, and I loaded up three big boxes into one of the carts and started down the dock. As I got to the corner and tried to make the turn, one wheel went over the edge along with the top carton. I struggled to grab the other cartons and the entire cart went into the harbor. Everything floated under the docks.

People working on their boats began shuffling the cartons toward me with their boat hooks. Little by little I was able to salvage all the cartons before they completely saturated and sunk, and I also hauled the cart on to the dock. After hosing the cart, I returned it to Flagship where

I was told that my license to drive carts on the dock had been revoked. As this was said in a British accent, I wasn't sure if it was dry British humor, or if she was serious. I did know that already everyone in the charter community knew who I was.

I loaded all the wet linens and towels into the dinghy, and set off to find the laundry, which, I had been told, was over in Crown Bay. The dinghy had no seats, so I had to sit on the inflated pontoon and bounce dangerously across the bay. I was later to bounce right out of that dinghy, but that wasn't during my first week, thankfully.

While my laundry was being washed and dried, I decided to go shopping for some local art for the boat. I found a couple of mocko-jumbie dolls made with wire inside so I could manipulate their shapes. Mocko-jumbies are stilt walkers that are dressed colorfully and wear masks, and can be found at local carnivals, parades and festivals. I also bought a couple of paintings to replace the motel-like décor on *Serene*, which was the name of my sailboat.

One day when I was scrubbing and cleaning, I noticed that the kitchen sink did not drain properly. I thought it might be a problem with a filter again and looked below the sink where I saw a motor. I thought, "This would be a good thing to hook up to the sink to drain it, and traced the wiring up to a button, which read, "Drain." Okay, I thought, so great minds think alike.

Little by little, I was getting the boat ship shape, and still hadn't pickled the water maker, although I didn't need the water I was making, as I was hooked up to water on the dock.

Boats are terribly independent critters. They can make their own water and energy. After a hurricane when there is no power on shore, a boat like *Serene* has power, air conditioning and ice as long as she has diesel, and with a 650-gal tank, that would be for a long time. And when anchored in the bay, we were also safe from rats and cockroaches climbing aboard.

I did manage to do everything I wanted to ready the boat for boat show, and my son, the captain, arrived in time too. However, I don't think the charter brokers were too impressed with a mother and son team. We would have to earn their respect through good reviews from the clients, who were already on the books, when I bought the working boat.

RUNNING FROM A HURRICANE

IRENE M HUBBARD

"**W**HERE ARE YOU GOING TO hide?" was the constant question on everybody's lips when Hurricane Luis was approaching St. Thomas. My son Chris and I had only been in the sailboat charter business for six weeks, and we hadn't fixed everything on the boat yet, and hadn't even figured out why the engine kept stalling, although the captain practically lived in the bilge with the two hundred forty horsepower Perkins diesel and the engine manual. My son was twenty-three years old and a recent graduate of Massachusetts Maritime Academy, where he had majored in transportation, not engines. He could pack a commercial ship so there was no wasted space, and everything was secure and balanced. But we were only a sixty-eight-foot ketch sailboat with a troublesome engine, and a few missing parts, like the forward sail which was in for repairs, and the generator which had a part in the shop.

Hurricane Luis was east of us, traveling west, and we didn't know where it was going to turn north. We thought about anchoring in Hurricane Hole over on St John, but all the good spots had been taken in those finger inlets in the mangroves. We really only had one choice left, as we couldn't stay in St. Thomas in the harbor. We were going to have to cross the Caribbean Sea, with five other boats headed to Curaçao, and we only had a half hour to get ready.

I ran to the store because my mother always told me to buy batteries when there was a hurricane coming. I bought a battery-powered lantern, which became the only light we used, as we conserved use of the house batteries, given that we didn't have a functioning generator to recharge them should we deplete their power. We needed power for the bilge pump, as we had a slight leak around the packing gland of the drive shaft, and the bilge pump went off every five minutes, pumping seawater overboard.

Chris hauled the little dinghy and motor onboard but didn't have time to haul up the sixteen-foot hard-bottomed inflatable with the ninety horsepower on it, so we had to tow that.

Some might think it was foolhardy to plan a three day trip across the Caribbean Sea when we had never sailed offshore before — and didn't have any running lights to alert other ships of our direction, and didn't have a generator, or a jib sail, or charts, or an auto pilot, which meant we had to steer the whole two hundred and fifty miles. But, never having experienced a Caribbean hurricane, we thought it was wise to keep away from the projected path. We also thought we would be safe with the other boats that did have running lights and charts. We would sail as a group, and we would alert any boats we saw on the way by VHF radio that we were traveling without running lights, although we did have a light at the top of the mast.

As we set off from St. Thomas it was close to sunset. In the Caribbean, when the sun dips below the horizon, it is like a shade is drawn. Darkness descends quickly, which is why we were in a hurry to leave, as there were no navigation lights off St. Thomas. We sailed with our mainsail and mizzen sail, while also running the engine, and kept up with the other boats that had their full complement of sails. As we watched the lights of St. Thomas fade behind us, we could see the hazy glow of Puerto Rico on the right, and the sea was inky black and calm as we powered along. There were three of us, our chef was a young woman who rapidly became seasick and spent at least one day lying on the floor, in the middle of the main saloon, tanked on Dramamine.

Twenty-two hours out we were all still awake, listening to the other boats chatter on their radios. I heard one of them talk about when we got to Spanish Water, so I figured that was the harbor on Curaçao, to which we were headed. It was like a little band of friends out for some night sailing, and the sky was bright with stars without light pollution from any shore. It was then that the engine failed. Chris tried to fix it but burned out the starter motor in the process, and we didn't carry an extra one onboard.

We radioed ahead to TriWorld, a trimaran charter sailboat, and the captain, who had some weather software, said that he would get the coordinates of the hurricane and call us back in a half hour. During that half hour wait, I was very frightened. I didn't think the boat was that seaworthy. She was fine for the charter industry, but I would never want to expose her to heavy weather. We were so green. I had never experienced large waves or fierce winds. I was getting teary eyed with fear.

My son looked at me and asked, "Are you crying?"

I said, "Well yeah, I'm scared."

He told me we were going to be fine. It reminded me of the day his father died four years earlier. We were all at the hospital a long time because we were donating my husband's organs, and it took a full day to get the heart recipient to the operating room. Then they took my husband to harvest his organs and we left for home. My anxiety was extremely high, and I had been crying and pacing all day. Once I got into the car between my two sons, I said, "I feel safe for the first time today."

And my nineteen-year-old son said, "That you are."

Tri-World's captain called back and reassured us that we were far enough south of the hurricane that we shouldn't get any of the bands. We relaxed and began life at sea. During the day I read an almanac of the Caribbean, which I had purchased for the boat. It listed the latitude and longitude of the lighthouse off the east end of Curaçao and showed Spanish Waters just around the point. We had a heading. Chris had blank chart paper and drew Curaçao roughly, starting with the lighthouse, and we plotted our passage across the Caribbean Sea, hourly, using the GPS.

Nights were gorgeous with the star-filled sky and the chirping of the dolphins, who would accompany us for an hour at a time. We had a flying fish land on the deck looking as befuddled as a fish out of water, and one little brown bird landed at our feet in the cockpit, probably all tuckered out from battling the hurricane someplace northeast of us, and we gave him some water and carefully avoided stepping on him, while he rested for an hour. At some point we lost all our wind and just drifted. I set up the hammock between the forestay and the main mast, and rigged the tiny windsurfer sail, as a forward sail, thinking any wind we could catch was a plus.

Chris decided to tow the fifty-ton vessel with the dinghy, and that was how we pulled the transom loose from the rest of the dinghy, so that it took on water. It wouldn't sink but was a larger drag on the boat when we towed it.

We were all awake in the cockpit watching lightening course around the boat when Chris said, "I wonder if there is any wind in those clouds?" I had no sooner responded,

"What clouds?" when we were hit with forty-five knots of wind and the boat heeled over greatly. I ran forward to make the main sail smaller, and Chris ran ahead to take down the rope hammock that was now set like a sail, and the screaming windsurfer sail. When I released the halyard, the line that holds up the sail, the boom came crashing down on the Bimini top, which was the canvas and frame covering the cockpit. I thought that was strange, because there is a line called the topping lift which holds up the boom when the sail isn't doing so. But that had snapped during the period of no wind, as the boom had been clanging from one side of the boat to the other. I tried to make the sail super small but couldn't as it was only rigged with one reefing line. The sail was lowered, and then wrapped to the boom and tied down. I couldn't make it as small as it could go, had it been rigged properly.

Chris and I returned to the cockpit and huddled out of the wind. My heart was beating so strongly I thought it might break a rib. When lightening hit, I would look at the waves and the foam, and whether or not it was streaming off the tops of the waves, as a way to measure the strength of the wind. I had been reading up on that, too, in my resource books.

The mainsail developed a five by two-foot rip that was flapping like a pennant. We watched that tear saying, "It's not getting any bigger, is it?"

Finally, Chris relinquished his, stingy, electric-sparing hold on our power, and decided to turn on the radar to see if there was an end to this white squall. It showed up as a line squall and we were almost through it.

After the storm, we had wind again, and we were about thirty-six hours from our destination, but none of us could sleep. Finally, we could see the light towards which we were heading, but it was dark and without charts, we didn't know if there were any reefs offshore. Chris had been to Curaçao on the Patriot State, Mass Maritime's sea class-rooms, and did not remember any reefs offshore, only close in to shore. We kept our heading and cleared that light about a half mile offshore. As dawn harkened, we could see the shore, nasty with reef and surf.

We dropped our sails and started to tow the boat, with the water-filled dinghy, into the harbor. After anchoring, the first thing we did was dinghy over to one of our friends and get some coffee, as we had run out days earlier. Then we went ashore to call home and let my other children and the cook's parents know that we were fine, in spite of being listed missing by the Coast Guard. I learned that my daughter was on first name basis with the Coast Guard, who contacted her frequently for the last two days. The trip took us five days instead of the usual three.

Hurricane Luis went north over St. Martin taking out two thousand boats. Five days after we arrived in Curaçao the eye of Hurricane Marilyn went over St. Thomas taking every red roof with it.

The power lines looked like licorice melted on the roads. The anemometer at the airport blew off in a gust measuring two hundred and twenty mph. It was a shock to return by water and see a blue island replacing the red tiled roofs on St. Thomas. The leafless, roofless island was covered in blue FEMA tarps.

A PHILOSOPHY OF AGING

Irene M Hubbard

I CAN'T HAVE DENTAL IMPLANTS BECAUSE my sinuses are sagging. They now sit right above the roots of my upper teeth. I can crown and bridge, but not implant. I marvel at all the people now getting dental implants. For me, everything has lost its springiness, and has drooped. I am lucky I have dense, fibrocystic breasts, or they would be under my belt.

Tinnitus is fun. Often, as you lose hearing, you gain a buzzing sound in your ears. It's great for sleeping; like your own private white noise machine. Now, my right ear has started to actually ring, like an iPhone from the next room. Not all the time, but often enough that I have begun to think of some lyrics for it.

Hearing loss reminds me of playing *Mad Libs*. That's the game where you ask for random nouns, adverbs, adjectives and verbs to fill in blanks in a story, and then read it back to the group. I am always mishearing words and experience non-sequiturs as a result. Some of them are hilarious.

Aging is the habit of saying goodbye. Goodbye to slimness, good looks, career, unimpaired eyesight, lubricated joints, muscle strength, agility, speed of movement, teeth, invincibility, firmness, fearlessness, and intestinal fortitude. It is hello to experience, gray hair, baldness, memory loss, arthritis, and chronic diseases. One thing that never changes, thank God for small favors, is our fingerprints. I was fingerprinted in elementary school, the whole school was, and today my fingerprints are as slim and perky as always, and can be identified from some national database, if I ever need reassurance about who I am.

There are two parts to my philosophy of aging. One part has to do with planning ahead. We are all told to plan for our elder years by saving in a retirement fund but that only addresses finances. To thrive in old age, it is a good idea not to put everything in one basket. If the basket breaks, as things tend to do the older we get, you lose all your eggs. So, the secret is to weave a lot of baskets in life, like hobbies and interests, family and friends, abilities and expertise, and not just focus on the development of one aspect of life, like work, or parenthood.

The second part of my philosophy is that I believe we become more like ourselves as we age. Not physically, but emotionally. Our neuroses have had ages to set and become durable. If part of our habit has been to work on our neuroses and try to mitigate them, then we are still working on ourselves into old age. If we had been more accustomed to putting our heads in the sand to avoid addressing issues, than the holes become deeper.

I have always been interested in the unconscious and what motivates people, and particularly what one can do to better herself. I wanted to examine what holds me back and exorcise it. Writing has helped me clarify some things that I have struggled with since I was a youngster.

I have been writing letters all my life. Growing up before the Internet, and living away from family, with long distance phone calls costing what they did, I wrote a lot of letters every week. The recipients told me that some of them were handed around for other people to read and one was framed and hung on the wall in my uncle's house. Some, like the letters to my mother-in-law, were ignored for fifteen years. But that didn't stop me from writing to her weekly.

As a teenager, I wrote epistles to my summer friends, whom I wouldn't see all winter, and received epics in return. As a married adult, I wrote love letters to my parents, which I'm sure embarrassed them, as they didn't speak that language.

I even enrolled in a home writing course that was called *The Famous Writer's Course*. They sent me an unabridged dictionary after I paid for the whole course up front. My husband called it our six-hundred-dollar dictionary, as it was never depreciated by my following through with the lessons.

I have been in a writing group for almost three years and the two group leaders have encouraged me to write a blog. We do twenty-minute writing exercises from a prompt and I usually write about myself and complete a whole story in the allotted time. I did go so far as to buy space on wordpress.com, for a blog. It is up for yearly renewal again.

We writers are among the fortunate aging folk. We do not depend on physical prowess for fulfillment in our lives, as the body surely declines with age. We can write even if we can't hold a pen anymore, as we can dictate. Stephen Hawking only had the use of an eye muscle to indicate letters, words and phrases, and he wrote books.

For the elderly accomplishments, I would rank writing right up there with ping pong and swimming. Maybe badminton.

A SEANACHAÍ

AN ENGLISH SCHOOL

Mary Clare O'Grady

MISS PLIMBLETTS WAS A VERY large androgynous creature. Her straight hair was cut close to her head, emphasizing her elephantine ears. The color of her hair was nondescript, as was the rest of her, devoid of color. Her British tweed suits were boxy, not really brown, not really grey - perhaps they just needed a good washing. The skirt ended below her knees, showing muscular calves falling into sturdy ankles and very large feet. Her brown oxford shoes, firmly coming down the linoleum hallway towards us, could easily have fit a man.

She didn't address us, or acknowledge our presence, just reached over the tiny heads bobbing around under her outstretched hand, unlocked the classroom door, and pushed it open. I clung to my mother, who was trying to convince me it would be okay, although her eyes told me she was not entirely comfortable leaving me with this primary school teacher.

Without a word, Miss Plimbletts offended my mother's American sensitivities, snatching me from her arms and placing me on the floor in the classroom. Then, bending at the waist, she placed her oversized hand on the middle of my small back and, with a push, sent me towards the others before she closed the door on my mother.

"In your seats!" she commanded, as if speaking to a room of adults. We were not used to being spoken to in such a manner. The whole idea of being in a classroom was a new concept.

She stiffly moved to the front of the room, as if she was one of those wooden dolls where the only movable joints were the shoulders and hips. Turning to face us, her tight lips moved sharply, while the words emanating were calm, as one completely in control. "Open your books now."

The room was barren. The eggshell walls blended into the floor and ceiling, except where broken by the blackboard along one side, windows on the other. Large panes of glass were set into thick walls, as if in a cloister. It was like stepping back in time to 1610 in Lancashire County, England, when the school was built.

Miss Plimbetts resembled the school building: an impregnable fortress. Her age was difficult to ascertain, somewhere in that vast ghost land between being single and an old maid. Perhaps if she had married, or had children, she would have been kinder to us.

The school's purpose was to process 750 children through their assessments. The first level, in which I had landed, began at age five and ended at age seven. The second stage was completed when children were eleven years of age and took the "11 plus" test for secondary school. Miss Plimbetts took her job seriously and expected the thirty of us in her charge to succeed at all costs. She was relentless with her teaching methods, having us recite over and over until we memorized the lesson. Then she quickly moved on to the next topic, without comment or praise. She never left the front of the room, leering down at us, as if a court judge.

I sat with my three neighborhood playmates, Shirley, Andrew, and Robert. They were used to my American accent and dress, but the other children and Miss Plimbetts considered me an oddity. Although we were all attired in the school uniform, my white saddle shoes and brightly colored coat stood in sharp contrast to the other student's dark oxfords and somber duffel coats.

The twins, Ailne and Avonne, were particularly British. They were square in build; their identical pale faces framed by black hair, cut as if a helmet had been placed on each of their heads. They equally enjoyed harassing all the other children, something Miss Plimbetts took no notice of - unless it interfered with the lesson or school policies. One day Ailne showed up with patent leather shoes. Miss Plimbetts was quick to admonish her and send her to the headmaster, emphatically stating to all of us, "Those shoes are banned, as they can reflect your knickers."

Recess was a welcome break from her sterile and claustrophobic classroom. When the bell rang, we ran for the door. Ready for us to become someone else's responsibility, she stood aside, gladly accepting her brief reprieve. We tumbled out into the hallway, ran for the stairs, and down to the back door. Outside was the tarmac for jump roping, or ball bouncing. Beyond, the grass field sloped down the hill to the sand box, slide, and swing set. Free from the ever-searching eyes of Miss Plimbetts, the twins felt free to terrorize us.

One day they tied me to the swing set with their jump ropes. Unable to move, I looked up the hill into the third-floor classroom window and saw the shadow of Miss Plimbletts. She seemed in another world, observing us from the tower above. Then the bell rang announcing the end of recess. Anxious to get back up the hill to the schoolhouse and not be reprimanded for being late, I struggled with the ropes but could not get loose. Panicking, as the other children swarmed to the back door, I yelled, "Help!" Andrew came running, grappled with the jump ropes, and got me untied. We ran up the hill, panting as we reached the building. Miss Plimbletts was standing just inside the door, holding it open as everyone filed in. Being the last one through she gave me an appraising look and said sternly, "It's not good to be tardy." Then she shut the door behind me as I scuttled up the steps away from her.

A STRANGE NEIGHBOR

MARY CLARE O'GRADY

MULLIGAN LANE HAD A STEEP incline. About a mile up, just before the sharp bend to the right, was our home. Its lower left corner was nestled into bedrock. They had to blast half of it away during the construction, but if you went down to the basement remains of it were still there. Wet and damp.

From the driveway steep stairs, made of railroad ties stacked into the hillside, led up to the front entrance. Inside sunlight streamed through ceiling to floor windows. The sliding glass doors in the living room accessed the patio; from the dining room they opened onto the backyard, rising up into the woods.

I loved being outside. Happy to wander alone amongst the trees for hours, I would conjure up imaginary friends. But there was one place I did not explore by myself. I only went there with my brother Sean. He was three years younger, but much more adventuresome.

The first time he took me there I was sitting on top of the craggy rock looking down at its disappearance into the foundation, when he peeked out from the shrubs behind me exclaiming, "I have something to show you!"

Turning around to face him I asked, "What is it?"

"You won't believe it, come on!" and he was off.

I hesitated; we weren't supposed to roam away without letting Mom know. Looking back at the house, I didn't see her. Then I ran off after Sean.

At the back edge of the property he pushed apart the bushes and motioned for me to follow. Being careful not to get caught on the briars, I emerged on the other side to find him pointing excitedly while his hushed voice announced, "Look, that must be Mrs. Pronsberger's!"

On the school bus we had heard stories of the crazy woman living alone in a haunted mansion. Here, a palace rose up in grandeur; although many of its floors, turrets, and windows were obscured by a towering European beech. Its arms drooped gracefully down, creating a curtain of deep green leathery leaves.

"Come on," Sean whispered, "we can hide in the tree," and he disappeared into the swaying branches.

I looked around. Thought about how we shouldn't be here. Then I went in behind him.

It was quiet and dark. There was no grass, just moist dirt. The huge trunk's light grey bark provided the only illumination. We walked around it to peer out between its limbs on the other side. There we had a clear view. Directly in front of us was a circular drive of crushed stone that disappeared behind the tower on the far right of the structure. Looking up to its top window, I thought I saw something move. Flit, just for a moment. A flash of white.

"What was that?" I murmured.

"Something moving…" Sean said slowly.

From the distance came the sound of gravel crunching under car tires. We stiffened. The noise grew louder.

"We have to go," I said grabbing Sean's arm and pulling him with me, back past the trunk, through the branches, into the brush, down the hill, across the patio, pushing the sliding door open, and scrambling inside.

"What are you two doing?" asked Mom.

"Nothing," we answered in unison.

Dinner that night started off as it always did, with Dad saying grace, but ended rather strangely. Our plates were almost empty when something caught my eye in the glass behind Dad, a white shape moving down the hill towards us.

A woman was standing in the backyard wearing a slip that fluttered softly around her with the breeze.

"Is that Mrs. Pronsberger?" Mom asked incredulously.

Sean and I shifted in our seats nervously.

"I'll go see," said Dad pushing his chair back. He climbed the hill until his fully dressed body, looking uncomfortable, stood next to her half-clad figure.

Mom, trying to divert our attention from the woman's underwear, said, "Pass me your empty plates."

"Mom why is she only wearing…", started Sean.

A *swish* came from the door opening and Dad reappeared.

"What did she want?" we all sang out, as if in a chorus.

"Oh, it was nothing, Mrs. Pronsberger just came by to say hello. I'm going to put the kettle on for tea."

"I'll get the dessert," said Mom and followed him into the kitchen.

Across the table Sean's eyes widened, "That was weird…"

I nodded, "Very strange."

THE PUNISHMENT

MARY CLARE O'GRADY

MY ARMS ARE WRAPPED AROUND the porcelain bowl, head lolling against my left elbow. There's knocking on the bathroom door and from the other side my mother's startling voice, "What are you doing? You've been in there a long time!" Lifting my head, I push my feet against the cold tile floor. As I rise the room starts to spin. I reach out to the countertop, brace myself, and close my eyes.

Earlier I was out with high school friends. Most Saturday evenings our senior year we gathered around a bonfire, back in the woods off Route 27, beer in hand, but on this night we went to the McMillan's. With their parents out of town it was a perfect place to gather. The McMillan kids loved to party, set up a bar in their parent's den and served pretty drinks - pink lemonade and vodka. They tasted sweet and slid down easily.

I'm not sure how I get home, but I do remember climbing the stairs to our back door. Holding onto the banister tightly, with each step I will my feet to stay beneath my swaying body. At the top I hesitate and take a deep breath before turning the doorknob. Stepping into the den, where Mom is watching T.V., I avoid her eyes. "Hello," I say and quickly cross the room to get upstairs, feeling her eyes on my body.

"Are you o.k.?" she asks.

Looking at the stairs in front of me I mutter back to her, "Yeah, I'm just tired, going to bed," hoping she doesn't notice any slurred words.

I don't recall getting up to my bedroom, undressing, or getting into bed, but suddenly I am alert – and not in a good way. I feel sick and dash to the bathroom to retch. Then I doze off until Mom knocks on the door.

Her voice has risen a decibel and is now slightly hysterical, "Mary, open this door!"

I force my eyes to focus on the door handle, turn it, and pull inwards.

"Look at me," she says sternly; her eyes exuding scorn, "you should be ashamed of yourself. It's the middle of the night, go back to bed."

"I will, I just have to go the bathroom," I mumble, lying so that I can close the door between us. Alone again I stare at the bedraggled creature in the mirror, take a deep slow breath, wash my hands, and rinse out my mouth. Shutting off the fluorescent light I emerge into the hallway. It is dark and I place my right hand on the wall to steady myself and slowly advance to my bedroom.

Another knock, gentler, and Dad's voice, "Mary, can I come in?"

Opening my eyes, I find sunlight streaming through my bedroom window and am pleased that this room is not spinning. "Yes, come in," I say and roll over to face him, then cringe with a sudden pain that splices through my head, forcing my eyes shut.

"How do you feel?"

"I'm okay," I say, sounding like some sort of animal from deep underground.

"Well, you've learned your lesson. Now you know that O'Grady's can't handle much liquor. Your mother is very upset. She's worried about you. You should go downstairs and eat something."

"Okay," I croak, then hear the door shut softly and ponder how someone with a name like O'Grady can't drink.

I move slowly pulling on my bathrobe. My slippers pad down the stairs, across the hall, and pause in the kitchen doorway. Mom, her back to me, fusses in the sink. My younger brothers and sister sit around the table finishing their cereal. They look up at me and stare, as if they don't know who I am. Our mother, feeling my presence, turns and glances at me briefly, with disgust, then looks back to the window above the sink in front of her.

Sensing the tension, the three at the table hurriedly empty their bowls, deposit them on the countertop, and disappear. Slowly I step into the kitchen, "Mom, I'm sorry." There is no response. It is as if I am not there. She lifts the bowls from the countertop, rinses them, puts them in the dishwasher, and moves into the laundry room. I hear the dryer open and envision her folding crisp white sheets.

I take a bowl from the cabinet, pour cereal in, cover it with milk, and sit down with a spoon. The only sound I hear is the crunching in my mouth.

My mother returns with a basket of clean clothes. Her look is pained, disappointed. I try again, "Mom, I'm sorry," but I see the look on her face, horrified that a daughter of hers could behave in such a way, dismayed at it all. She is at a complete loss. Without looking at me, she shakes her head and passes into the front hall and upstairs.

Sitting alone in the quiet kitchen, my parent's soft arguing drifts down the stairs. My mother's voice is upset and insistent, "Surely there must be some punishment, grounded for a month maybe...." My father's response is calm and firm, "She has already been punished enough."

He must have won because there is no grounding, or any other punishment, except for the brutal silence from my mother for days afterwards.

THE FIRE

Mary Clare O'Grady

IT HAD BEEN LIKE ANY other winter day on the campus of Providence College. Darkness fell early, finals were scheduled, and studying was ferocious. So, when the snow began to fall that night, it lightened everyone's mood. Many donned mittens and hats and ran outside to the quad, releasing tension by throwing snowballs at each other and getting soaked. It wasn't until long after midnight that things quieted down, and those mittens and hats were hung to dry, as their owners fell into their beds.

I was woken by the lights. Red, white, and yellow - beating rhythmic yet scary patterns on the window shade that separated the quad from our dorm room. My roommate and I grabbed something to throw over our pajamas and opened our bedroom door. Mass chaos erupted in the hallway outside. A girl ran by, "There's been a fire in Aquinas Hall, they're bringing some of the rescued girls here." We followed her through the swinging doors separating our dorm rooms from the lounge.

Entering the room, hysteria ruled. Young women in pajamas were crying, moaning, and screaming. They weren't coherent. I didn't know what to say. Through the windows the quad was a sea of lights, policeman, and fireman. The darkness of Aquinas Hall loomed down on us.

I turned back to the girls, none of whom I knew. They were hugging each other, while I stood helpless, not knowing what to do.

I felt an urgent need to talk to my mother, my father, but the phone lines were jammed. Hours passed. Back in my room, I dressed and followed everyone else to the cafeteria as a new day began.

It was light outside, but it was wet. The spray from the fire trucks had soaked the now gaping dark windows of Aquinas Hall. Water had flowed down its walls and soaked into the snow, revealing the grass and dirt beneath. Students, emerging from the surrounding dorms, progressed slowly and quietly towards breakfast. Hushed comments moved through the crowd.

"Did you see the ambulances that took some girls away?"

"I heard that ten girls died."

"One of them jumped to her death on the sidewalk."

"The fireman told her to wait."

Awful stories.

Inside Raymond Cafeteria things appeared to be as they always had. The chef in his big white hat, the serving ladies with their hair up in those nets; but it was different, no one checked our meal card at the door, no one was laughing, and there were no attempts at a food fight. Everyone filed in quietly, picked up a tray, and got in line. I lifted a plastic pastel colored plate from the pile. It popped as it separated from rest, still moist from the dishwasher. I slid my tray along the two steel bars in silence. Across the counter, those in the kitchen seemed as ill at ease as we did, silently scooping the bland food onto our plates, without the usual banter between staff and students.

Sitting down amongst friends, I felt a little better. We talked of the mass that Father Peterson, the President of the College, had just announced. It would be held in the gym, a space big enough to hold all who wanted to attend. I rarely went to mass anymore, but now it was somewhere to go, something to do.

As we walked across campus the crowd grew, but the only sound was whispers. Inside the gym, it filled, and filled, and filled. A sense of warmth began in my belly and rose up into my chest. Tears came for the first time, and a sense of relief.

We sat there, hoping to be the person we were yesterday, but Father Peterson talked to us about how we were all now changed; we needed to embrace that, and take it with us. An opportunity, perhaps, to live differently, because this horrible thing had taken ten of us away. We left changed. Acutely aware that we had the rest of our lives to live - for ourselves and for those now gone.

Mom picked me up from campus. I left as if in a bubble. Disconnecting from something that had brought so much confusion and fear, then meaning and clarity; I was unable to communicate my feelings. I had little to say during the forty-five-minute car ride. At home, surrounded by my family, I could not find the words to relate what I had experienced. I wanted to share it with them, but it was too hard.

So, I went upstairs to my bedroom and lay down until I was called to dinner.

AN ULTIMATUM

MARY CLARE O'GRADY

IT WAS MY TENTH COLLEGE reunion weekend that blew it all open. We were there with my girlfriends and their husbands. We girls had been tight since college, and the guys had grown to enjoy each other's company just as much. Over the four years that Eric and I dated, the eight of us shared a lot of good times together. There were the nights out in Boston, ski weekends in New Hampshire, dinners in each other's homes, and the weddings. We had been present at each of their weddings.

The reunion took place on a spring day at Providence College. Afterwards, we said our goodbyes and headed off in different directions. Eric and I had fallen into a pattern of alternate weekends at my condo in Arlington, Massachusetts and his bungalow in Newport, Rhode Island. The later was our base that weekend and during the forty-minute drive back we laughed about the antics that one or the other of the group had pulled over the course of the day.

Something changed once we got back to the house. What was said that caused the scene I do not remember. But it definitely involved the subject of marriage. This wasn't the first time it had come up. We were no spring chicks, I was thirty-two, he forty-four. Yeah, it's a pretty big age difference, but I had always been the older mature kid and he was a child at heart, so we met in the middle.

The real issue was that he had been married before, many years before. The divorce had been one of those nasty brutal affairs that leaves deep scars. As a result, here he was almost twenty years later, with a portfolio of past girlfriends, and an intense aversion to ever marrying again. It wasn't until much later that I realized how much it terrified him.

Before we met I had been in no rush to wed; concentrating on establishing my career, getting my master's degree, and traveling without appendages. But that had all been accomplished by the time of the reunion. Being on campus with my married friends may have accentuated the fact that we were not. Or it could have been my frame of mind at that time. In any event, I brought the subject up. And again, he answered, "Why can't we just live together?"

I was raised Catholic. I didn't go to church anymore, hadn't in years, but something from that upbringing had filtered through and gotten wedged inside me. I was fine with anyone else who wanted to live together, but it wasn't for me. I love tradition and wanted a ceremony with a long white gown, "...in sickness and in health...," surrounded by those I love.

So, we had a fight. Or I had a tantrum. I left in a huff. Getting into my Toyota Corolla and revving the engine, I peeled out of the driveway and headed towards the highway for Boston. Halfway there I realized I had left my dress hanging on the door of his closet. Perhaps my subconscious had planned this? I debated with myself over what to do, then turned the car around and raced back to Newport slamming into his driveway.

He initially looked pleased to see me, then stood aside as I mumbled that I had forgotten the dress, pushed into the house to get it, and escaped with squealing tires. Did I want him to chase after me like Prince Charming? Yes. Alas, no such luck.

After several years of spending weekends together, it was hard to break that routine, but before leaving Newport I let Eric know that I couldn't continue to spend time together without the commitment I needed from him. I just couldn't do the dating thing anymore. I said, "By the end of the year we agree to marry, or it is over." There, it was done. An ultimatum delivered.

It was what I needed to do, but in doing so I also destroyed the joy that had been in my heart. I was sad all the time, cried a lot, wrote a lot of letters - never sent, thank God. I didn't sleep well, couldn't finish a meal, had an upset stomach for weeks, and lost a lot of weight. I managed through the workday by spending lunch breaks at one of Boston's city parks. There I would read from the Bible, something I had never done before, but somehow Psalm 23 made me feel better. Coming home I would anxiously open my door, looking for a blinking light on the phone, to find none. It was a dark period.

I forced myself to move on. I made plans with single friends to go out on Friday and Saturday nights. On Saturday mornings I took the T to Faneuil Hall and the Farmer's Market where my purchases always included flowers to bring home. On Sundays I walked down to Quebrada's, the local bakery, and brought back one of their delicious scones or muffins, or both, to relish with coffee. I joined a single's outing club and went on bike riding weekends to Stowe, Vermont and Block Island, Rhode Island. I told myself that if I never heard from him again, I could live my life alone.

He called. He was at his buddy Mike's in New Hampshire and suggested we meet at Crane Beach in Gloucester, Massachusetts the next day. "Yes, okay," I said, beyond happy, while trying to contain my excitement.

It was a beautiful summer day. I drove up full of anticipation. Finding each other on the beach we were suddenly awkward. Neither of us seemed to know what to say. We made small talk. We laid a blanket down on the sand and soaked up the heat of the sun and the closeness of our bodies. After a couple of hours, I got tired of the chit chat and asked, "What are we doing here?"

Taken aback by the question Eric replied, "I just thought we could get together."

Upset, I moved quickly, picking up my things and moving through the sand dunes to my car. How could he think it would be fine to just hang out, like friends? My feelings for him were so much stronger than that, I needed so much more from him, that I couldn't settle for less.

He followed, wanting to talk.

I drove away.

After that, communication was sparse. He called every once in a while, to see how I was doing. I tried to stay strong, making my own plans, while waiting for my self-imposed year-end deadline. Christmas approached. We would each be spending it with our own families, me in New York, him in Virginia, but agreed to meet before the holiday.

We sat on my sofa and exchanged gifts. I have no recollection of what I gave him, but he gave me a beautiful piece of stained glass, a pair of Birkenstocks, and a cigar....

What's this?" I asked. He turned very pale. His hands were shaking as he pulled the band from the cigar and put it on my finger.

"What, are you… doing?" I asked, then realized, but had to be sure. "What is this?" I asked shakily.

He answered in a trembling voice, with a question, "Will you marry me?"

I started crying, tears of joy.

A DIFFERENT KIND OF FAMILY

MARY CLARE O'GRADY

I HAVE NEVER BEEN A MOM, although technically I am a stepmother.

My Mom recently said to me, "I loved being a mother," with such wistful emotion that I thought she was going to cry. She has devoted her life to that role, wanting nothing more than the warmth of a family of her own. She succeeded. After marrying early, she raised a brood. Fulfilling the quintessential role of her times, she did not work, but stayed home to cook, clean, take care of her off-spring, and please her husband. Not a bad gig, based on who her husband and kids were.

As children, we were surrounded by immediate and extended family members, all with pale skin and blue eyes. They were involved in every aspect of our lives, fiercely espousing their closest held values - religion and education. Our great aunts, uncles and grandparents, who had to leave school at fourteen for jobs to help out their families, strongly encouraged us to take advantage of as much schooling as possible. Advanced degrees were held in high esteem. As for religion, if we obeyed the rules of the Catholic Church, we would be happy for eternity. It was understood that later in life we would marry, in that faith, and it would be for life.

When I was in elementary school, I wanted six kids (including some adopted from other countries). In junior high, I decided four of my own would be better (two girls and two boys). Then, in high school, I wondered if three might be easier. By college age I thought about adding a career to that package. I figured I could successfully achieve a rewarding work life, while simultaneously raising a family of my own – if I had just two kids. When I met my husband, we agreed on maybe having one child. In the end I had none.

Mom must have wondered why, but she has never asked. I assume she was disappointed; her first child, eldest daughter, not sharing in the most important aspect of her life. Perhaps that is why neither of us have ever brought it up.

However, on several occasions she did raise the subject of my getting married. Her appeals became more desperate when I was in my late twenties. She appeared concerned by my independent freedom, how much I was enjoying living the single life, and was clearly worried about the lack of a man on the horizon. To assure her that I was fine without a man, I said, "Mom, there's so much I want to do first, I don't even want to think about getting married until I'm at least thirty."

"Don't say that!" she cried out, frightened by my boldness, unable to grasp such a line of thinking.

I, however, persevered. Working toward my goals, I found like-minded single people my age, joined a Vermont ski house for winter weekends, then a summer rental in Newport, Rhode Island. That was where I met the man I would marry.

I can clearly picture telling Mom about him. We were in my condo in Arlington, Massachusetts. Hanging curtains in my bedroom window I looked outside, not at her, thinking she would not be pleased with the much older Protestant man that I had fallen for. I took a deep breath, and spoke slowly, "Well... he's older. Not Catholic. Divorced. Has a couple of kids." Then I stood very still, anticipating an avalanche of despair to hit me. Instead, a crescendo of joy spilled out of her. She was delighted, either because she trusted my instincts, or was thrilled to have me finally married off at thirty-three.

My marriage resulted in an instant family, although nothing like the one I had sprouted from. My two stepdaughters are not pale, their eyes brown; one resembles their father, the other their mother - who remarried when the girls were young, converted to Judaism, and raised them in that faith.

Their weddings were happy occasions, where my husband proudly walked them up to the Huppah (a canopy under which the Jewish couple stand during their wedding ceremony). When my first step-grandchild celebrated her Bat Mitzvah, I sat in temple amazed and proud, as she recited long memorized passages from the Torah in Hebrew.

My stepdaughters, their husbands, and children have become an integral part of my life. While differences have not stopped us from growing close, they do not think of me in terms of a motherly figure.

They were entering their twenties when I first came into their lives, and it took some time for us all to adjust to the fact that I was closer in age to them, than I was to their father. They stumbled with introducing me as "My stepmother," saying instead, "This is my Dad's wife, Mary Clare." Their children also call me by my first name, instead of one of the many versions of Grandma - like "Nanny," which my mother's grandchildren affectionately call her.

The family I grew up in, the one I assumed I would replicate, is not the one I inhabit today. Choices made along the way have brought me to a different place. Because of others, it is full of love. Yet occasionally, a sentimental moment will hit me, when I think back to my experiences as a child and the comforting sense of sameness - which has dissipated into a world of accepting differences.

A SEANACHAÍ

Mary Clare O'Grady

I FEEL CLOSER TO HIM NOW than when he was alive. His words breathe on the hundreds of pages he left behind, opening doors for glimpses into other lives.

My Great Uncle Paddy was a thin-boned small man, not much larger than myself. The shine on his bald head was almost as bright as the light that danced in his blue eyes. He had a smile that never left his face, his happiness contagious. Unable to stand or sit still for very long he had an enormous appetite for life and adventure, borne out of an uneducated childhood of desperate poverty living in a country occupied by foreigners. Yet he traveled the world, on a tanker delivering Guinness brew to ports across the globe.

He was known as a teller of fantastic stories. On the rare occasion that he would, as he called it, "Pop across the pond to America," or when my family made one of our very few trips to the Emerald Isle, he told us tales: his father eloping to marry a first cousin, British raids on their home, and his sister's eight year old son who shot and killed her in the Australian Outback. On these handful of brief encounters, I did not know whether to believe his amazing stories or not, so I laughed them off.

A few years after he passed away, I came to believe them all.

I had begun to work on a family tree. Over time, it branched out to include over a thousand souls going back many generations. Family members were in awe of what I had uncovered, while barely able to contain their amusement over my obsession with it all. During my research I discovered that all he had told us was true. He had not been telling "tall tales" after all. It took my breath away – and drew me further in. Searching for more, I visited the home of his son Sean and wife Gaye, in the Wicklow Mountains.

"He thought the world of you," they told me.

"He did?" I asked dumbfounded, amazed that a great uncle I had seen so infrequently had given me much thought.

"Oh yes, and he'd be so pleased to know that you were here in this kitchen with us now."

I was overwhelmed by their comments.

Uncle Paddy spent his final days in that house, leaving behind boxes and boxes and boxes of his journals, a treasure trove of stories. Looking through them, I realized he had clearly been our family's Seanachaí, that is Irish for those who bring old stories to life and keep track of important information for their clan, holding the key to their culture's past and its most important memories and traditions.

I was only in the house for a few days. Time pressed down on me as I carefully lifted the pages from the boxes, read, and photocopied.

About his childhood he wrote, "All together eight, Bill, Mary, Larry, Bridie, Annie, Jimmy, John, and me Paddy, the 'shakings of the bag,' living in two bedrooms with a bucket on the landing for you know what... My older brothers... carrying messages and guns... My father... intelligence...

for the IRA... leading to many raids on our home by the dreaded Black and Tans."

He wrote about spending summers on his grandparent's farm, "People were far better off in the country... When I arrived, I was given a donkey, a .22 rifle, and a fishing rod... had the time of my life... fresh rabbit, trout, and pheasants... will never forget the food, fresh air, and freedom."

Then there was the story about his mother's funeral. "We transferred her body from the upstairs bedroom to the parlor downstairs. Got help from... a neighbor, a very nervous chap scared... of corpses. Between us we carried Mother down the stairs, maneuvering her around the bend, when suddenly a loud long fart could be heard. The poor neighbor nearly had a seizure. Then Mother's sister arrived and turned every picture and mirror to the wall and stopped all the clocks, as a very superstitious woman."

These stories occupy my mind, which spends a lot of time in the past, a past before I existed, where people and events appearing dark and mysterious, intrigue me. I work to bring them into the light, to imagine what their lives were like, and understand why they made the decisions they did.

I spend a couple of hours most days squirreled away in my studio, furiously writing down words, then moving them around, until inserting another one entirely - desperately trying to portray their lives vividly and hoping to do them justice, as far flung from my reality as they are.

Uncle Paddy, who sure could 'spin a yarn,' has awakened in me some dormant storytelling gene.

HOME ON THE RANGE

BARBED WIRE AND CATTLE GUARDS

Judith Porter

I GREW UP IN A GHOST town. Well, more like a pseudo ghost town. The ghosts were hanging around when I lived there, but it wasn't until we moved away, just before my senior year in high school, that the whole place was dismantled and discarded, and ghosts took over.

Now the only way to find my old stomping grounds is to know where it was.

Carter Nine, Oklahoma, was an oil camp, which I suppose I should explain given that they no longer exist. When oil was discovered in the early 1900s, in Oklahoma, this led to a boom time in the quest for 'black gold.' Housing was needed for the large number of people caught up in this drilling frenzy.

One of the earliest and most notorious towns was DeNoya, otherwise known as Whizbang. This early lawless community thrived and died in the span of some twenty years. This camp grew haphazardly with bars, brothels, and gambling establishments popping up almost overnight. People were housed in tents, huts and other make-shift structures. A rough element of around ten thousand, mostly men, swarmed the area to make their fortune. Among Whizbang's early inhabitants was a roustabout named Clark Gable, long before he became a famous person for not giving a damn.

The lawlessness and disorder of this and other early oil boom towns was one of the reasons that the Carter Oil Company decided to create its own camp when they came into the area in 1924. The company started building about fifty houses with electricity and plumbing, for the most part. They fenced the whole area with barbed wire and provided cattle guards to prevent local herds from getting inside. In its heyday Carter Nine grew to around 500 houses, with a bunkhouse, a school, stores, offices, a post office, and a community hall. It was actually incorporated as a town in 1928.

By 1945, however, Carter Nine was on the downside of demise. There wasn't much left of its former glory. It had a small grocery store, a post office about the size of an outhouse, and the community hall, mostly unused. It no longer qualified as a town.

I was three years old when we arrived there after my dad was hired by Skelly Oil Company. Skelly had purchased the place from Carter Oil years before. Only about thirty families occupied the little houses that peppered the road. My dad called Carter Nine 'Malfunction Junction.'

My earliest memories are somewhat vague. There was a barbed wire fence surrounding the entire camp. And cattle guards. On the outside of each of our small houses were t-pole clothes lines, trash barrels, and broken sidewalks.

What we didn't have were asphalt roads, street signs, streetlights, house numbers, or locks and keys for our doors.

The yards all ran together with a combination of crab-grass, rock, and dirt. Nobody had a "lawn." Landscaping was not in our vocabulary. I don't remember flowers except for the sweet smell of a wild honeysuckle bush outside my bedroom window. There were a few peach trees bunched together in an open lot with hard-as-rock, worm-holed peaches. We used these for throwing rather than eating. We also had some other unsubstantial trees but, aside from offering us some much-need shade on Oklahoma-hot days, they weren't worth much.

Our house looked like everybody else's. It was wooden clapboard, rectangle, with six rooms and a bathroom. The left side of the house had a kitchen, dining room, and living room. Down the right side were three bedrooms with a bathroom stuck between.

There was also a porch in the back that we never used. In truth, the porch was the front of the house with the living room door as the front door, but that faced the barbed wire fence. Our comings and goings were through the kitchen. The dirt path in front of that door was where we parked our car.

The house had a single gas stove for heat, located in the dining room. Many a morning my brother and I pranced around that stove half-dressed trying to get warm enough to put on the rest of our clothes.

Our furniture was not memorable, except we had a woven rug made of paper in the dining room which I loved to mention to visitors. I think Mom got that unique possession from a Sears, Roebuck catalog. And we had a ceramic green rearing stallion lamp in the living room. Things like that you just don't forget.

What I loved about our house were the two galvanized cables about one-inch width that went over the roof in the front and in the back to hold the house down in the event of a tornado. I believed in those cables. It never occurred to me that they wouldn't actually work if a tornado struck, but fortunately, they were never tested to prove their worth one way or the other.

The oil company must not have had much faith in the cables because they equipped the camp with several cement storm cellars. These were solid structures rising about three feet above ground, shaped like a rooftop with no house below. A steel bulkhead door was attached on one end. When the skies became perilous, the night watchman would sound the company siren and we would run through the rain or hail to the cellar. Other than that, the cellars were a great place for 'king of the mountain' games.

There was a real town nearby where we were bused to school. Shidler was about three or four miles from Carter Nine. It was no great shake of a place, either, but it was far superior to the camp. As well as a school building, Shidler had paved streets, churches, some stores, a movie theater, and a stop sign. Shidler and Carter Nine were in Osage County, about halfway between Ponca City and Pawhuska.

I think I was about eight or nine-years-old when telephones were installed. They were wooden boxes attached to a wall in the house. They were equipped with a mouthpiece in the middle and a bell above it. The listening device hung on one side and a crank was on the other, for ringing people. It was a party line with others in camp and the bell rang every time anyone got a call. We were supposed to answer only when it was for us (one long and a short was our ring), but, on occasion, curiosity got the best of me.

I clearly remember the first television set to arrive. I was in fifth grade. The family that owned this curious device invited all the kids to watch *The Lone Ranger* at 4pm on Wednesday afternoons. Truth be told, I was terrified of this new contraption, so I stood in the kitchen with the women and peeked through to the living room.

Soon afterward, my dad bought us a television set and I was hooked. The black and white screen had about a 13-inch screen, knobs on the side to straighten the horizontal and vertical lines, and an antenna that didn't work. My dad put a bigger antenna on the roof so we could receive the two channels from faraway Tulsa. *Your Hit Parade, The Loretta Young Show, Jack Benny.* My world had opened up dramatically.

During the day we kids were a semi-feral group, left to our own devices once school was out. We freely roamed inside and outside the barbed wire fence playing without adult supervision.

I remember once when my brother Judd dislocated a shoulder trying to pole vault onto a shed. His foot got caught and he fell. His friends popped the shoulder back in place. Neither of us ever told Mom because he'd have been in big trouble. We were independent when we played outside, but we weren't supposed to be stupid.

In summer we went barefoot a good deal of the time, therefore our feet were heavily calloused and always stained brown with dirt. I don't remember ever worrying about the rough terrain, but I do recall how it felt to get stung by stepping on bees or prickly weeds.

With no stores to speak of, finding clothes was a problem. Twice a year we awaited the arrival of the Sears Roebuck catalog. It was a source of excitement and entertainment. Mom usually allowed us to order one outfit for school in September, and another outfit for Easter in the springtime. My brother and I canvassed the pages for the perfect item to satisfy our fashion desires. We changed our mind numerous times before settling on something affordable. My mom had a sewing machine and made some clothes for me, though I don't think she ever made anything for my brother.

We also received boxes of hand-me-downs from cousins or older friends. And on special occasions, we went to the big city of Tulsa on a shopping spree, mostly for shoes since it's hard to get the proper size by mail order.

While my dad had his job at the plant, I don't know what my mother did or how she survived those years, isolated as we were. Her days must have been challenging. There were plenty of chores, of course. Needless to say, Oklahoma's reputation for dust was readily apparent. My mother accepted the housekeeping challenge with a vengeance. She cooked all our meals and baked sweets for after school snacks. Mostly though, her days were filled with mediocrity.

Mom finally learned to drive when she was thirty-four-years-old which gave her an occasional escape from the barbed wire fences. But she was second in line for the car behind my dad, and when my brother learned to drive, she was third in line. Needless to say, I knew my place. I didn't learn to drive until I got to college.

The men were blue collar workers (except for the plant manager, a kind man with a bulbous red nose, who wore a white shirt and sometimes, even a tie). Our dads went to work in the morning when the siren went off and returned home at 5pm when the siren signaled the end of the work-day. They wore jeans, or khakis, or overalls and carried those black metal lunch boxes with rounded tops. They all wore hats, as was the style of the times, and most of them smoked cigarettes, pipes, or cigars—or, like my dad, all three at various times.

I wrote a couple of childhood friends to ask what memory stood out about living in Carter Nine. Marlene said, "I will never forget Lloyd Rafferty's grocery store. We would go there, and he would give us sacks and let us pick the berries from his mulberry trees. We would eat them from the trees every spring. Then one day my mom said we needed to wash them first. OMG! We couldn't believe the bugs that floated off of them. To this day, I hate mulberries."

Joe wrote, "On the bad side was seeing a man get crushed by a load of 4-inch pipes while unloading them from a truck onto a trailer, or seeing another truck driver literally cut in half when the load of pipe he was hauling shifted forward when he put on the brakes at the cattle guard. Also, the guy who blew himself up carelessly handling dynamite in the pipe yard." He added, "while these were troubling events, they forced the need to keep safety always in mind, as well as prepared my mind for the carnage I would witness in later life." (He was a Vietnam vet.)

Despite being country bumpkins in the middle of nowhere, my mother had her standards where I was concerned. I was not allowed to listen to country music, pierce my ears, or wear fringe, much to my chagrin. I was corrected every time I said 'git' instead of 'get.' I wore hats and gloves to church on holidays. I was a Rainbow girl. I was supposed to be a lady although my daily life was far from ladylike. When Mom blew the whistle at supper time, we came home dirty, sun burned, and full of the day's entertainment that often involved mud, wildlife, and the odd insect.

There was nothing scenic about our little part of the world. The land was flat. As Judd liked to say, "So flat you can look until your eyeballs hurt and never see the end."

I remember once there was an out-of-control prairie fire when I was about eight or nine-years-old. It started when some field hands left a large bottle of water on the back of a pickup truck. The water bottle acted as a magnifying glass as the sun burned through and started a fire in dry weeds nearby. Almost all the men in the plant fought the fire pounding the flames with dirt-filled gunny sacks. I remember standing outside the house and seeing a thin line of red golden flames across the whole horizon. My dad would come home dirty and stinking of smoke. He would eat, rest, and return for another shift. It took days to bring the fire under control.

In 1989 those fields became a national park called the Tall Grass Prairie Preserve, run by the National Conservancy. The preserve, nearly 40,000 acres in Kansas and Oklahoma, created the largest protected remnant of tall grass prairie on earth.

We had no idea our homeland was worthy of a national park when we were stuck in this wild, dry, remote place.

MY OLD TIME RELIGION

JUDITH PORTER

MY MOM'S FAMILY WERE MAJOR players in the Disciples of Christ, Christian Church. Mom was a church-goer from day one, so she felt it her responsibility to be sure my brother and I had that same religious experience every Sunday morning.

My dad's family was not closely acquainted with Sunday morning services, so he saw no reason to be. When Mom suggested he join us, he generally deferred, being a Methodist, or so he said. The only difference I knew between the Methodists and the Disciples of Christ, Christians was that the Methodists saved souls by sprinkling, and the Disciples of Christ, Christians dunked.

There were multiple Protestant churches in our little town of Shidler, Oklahoma, and one Catholic Church. I had one friend who was Catholic. I knew very little about her religion except she got to wear a doily on her head at mass. Frankly, I knew very little about any of the religious denominations except, according to my daddy, who was worldly and knew these things, Baptists, like Republicans, were not to be trusted.

His sentiment, however, did not prevent him or my mom from allowing me to attend Vacation Bible School with my best friend Linda at the Baptist Church at Carter Nine. While we had to travel into town to attend our own church, this little Baptist church was located just outside the fence, inside a house rather than a church building. I could walk there with Linda, which is probably why I was allowed to join her. I think I was six or seven years old, which was before my mom learned to drive, so summer activities were pretty much limited to what was available around camp.

Linda was a year older so she knew about things I had never dreamed could be, and she was quick to tell me. Angels had wings and flew in the nude, and dead people's hair continued to grow in the grave until it completely wrapped around the skull and bones. Linda was a marvel.

Baptist Vacation Bible School, on the other hand, was not. My enthusiasm was quickly dampened when Linda and I were separated on the first day due to our one-year age difference.

Bible school was a hodgepodge of activity, mostly involving coloring inside the purple lines of mimeographed pictures of Jesus Christ doing Christly things—feeding the multitudes, preaching on a mountain, and sitting with all the little children of the world—red and yellow, black and white, they were precious in his sight.

The Crayola's they provided were nothing but stubs—bits and pieces that had been tossed in an old coffee can. Although they may have smelled that same waxy smell of new bought ones, they were messy and got all over our fingers as we made such diligent efforts to color our sheets.

The teachers were eager, stone-faced women who thrived on telling long-winded Bible stories.

Playtime meant fifteen whole minutes of romping with Linda and screaming just to hear ourselves. Breaks also included homemade cookies and Kool-Aid, which was set out on the picnic table in the shade of a large tree.

Thus, the week dragged on, too much like real school, culminating on Friday with what the teachers termed a special treat.

"We're going to have a church service, like the grown-ups, only just for kids," one of the teachers told us, clapping her hands. "The preacher is even going to preach to us."

Even I had doubts that this event deserved any kind of enthusiasm.

I ended up in the front row with Linda directly behind me, right where she could put her shoes on the back of my shorts, which, naturally, she did.

After much ado about songbooks and sitting up straight, the Reverend's stout body appeared before us. I kept my eyes focused on his scuffed brown shoes with frayed shoestrings and his well-worn pant cuffs that were dragging the ground so that his heels were standing on them.

"Welcome God's children," he bellowed, causing all of us to look up and gasp. "We are gathered together," the Reverend began again. This time his voice was as soft as a cotton pillowcase. I was content to let the words pour over me. Not that I went so far as to pay attention, mind you. My mind was wandering off to wonderful places of mystery and intrigue far from Vacation Bible School.

For what seemed like hours, the Reverend words soothed me and kept me in my dream state, only to be interrupted occasionally when the force of his delivery caused spittle to spray onto my head.

"The Lord saves those who save themselves," he declared as he slammed shut the Bible. That knocked me back to attention. I glanced up in time to see him cuddle the great book into his pudgy hand and place it over his heart.

All us little kids were stunned into silent awe as his eyes made a careful scrutiny of his wayward sheep. That's what he called us. "And now, my wayward sheep, let us come forward and give our hearts to God," he said with that voice again as warm as a favorite relative. "As we sing our final hymn, let us step into the light of God's life and be saved forevermore."

I didn't know what the words meant, but there was comfort in this man saying them to me.

The song began, "On a hill far away, stood an old rugged cross."

"Be born again young brethren and give up your life of transgressions, for salvation is the only way," he shouted above the singing. "We'll wash away your sins," he promised.

I had plenty of sins that needed washing away. Whatever salvation was, it sure sounded good.

"Yes, yes, dear little children come to me."

The song continued, "Where a world of lost sinners was saved."

I looked around. Kids were doing it. Kids were actually stepping forward. They were being saved right there before my eyes.

I wanted to be saved, too.

"Won't you come now?" the gentle voice asked.

I was standing very still, heart thudding wildly, when Linda stepped forward into that circle of saved souls. One minute she was behind me and the next minute she was up there with the preacher, right level with his Bible.

Linda was saved.

As the last verse was being sung two more kids came forward, but it still wasn't enough for the Reverend. "Come now," he pleaded. "Salvation will wash away your sins."

Salvation must have washed away reason because suddenly my feet led me forward, right up beside Linda.

I was sure my sins were escaping my tiny body out my ears and mouth and eyes and I was free.

"You're not supposed to be here," Linda growled through gritted teeth. "You ain't Baptist."

Baptist? Lordy, were you supposed to be Baptist to be saved? Nobody told me that. "I, I," I stammered, but no more words would materialize.

"You don't belong." Linda hissed.

I glanced down at my chair, wondering if I could slip back in it. But the Reverend was touching the top of my head with his fat fingers. In a matter of seconds my euphoria had been blown to bits by an even greater emotion. Shame. Nothing can crush the soul out of a kid faster than when she realizes she's made a terrible mistake in front of an audience of her peers. There was no escape. I gulped and stared down at my shoes. All I had wanted was that wonderful feeling. I wanted to rid myself of the sins of the world which had not only returned to me as rapidly as they had left but had now multiplied because I had committed an even greater sin than any that had come before.

I had become a Baptist.

I stuffed my hands in the pockets of my shorts and crumbled the bits of lint I found inside. I dared not look at anybody, especially Linda. Linda was tapping her foot and I could feel the heat steaming off her arm. I had a feeling, quite accurately in fact, that Linda was ripped because I had not only falsified my salvation; I'd somehow spoiled hers, too.

The good preacher turned to his saved sheep. He thrust his hand forward moving from child to child, clutching at our hands and congratulating each one warmly. I had no choice but to pull my hand from the protection of my pocket and reach it into his immense palm and fingers.

Next he invited the whole Bible School to come forward and welcome these saved sheep into God's family.

They did.

I thought I was going to die.

Every unwashed, sticky, accusing little hand shook mine, and every nasty little set of eyes stared me into further humiliation. Not even the invitation for cookies and more red Kool-Aid could hold me a minute longer in that terrible place. "I have to go now," I said quietly as the teacher gave me a mouthy kiss on the cheek.

I went home mortified that I'd mucked up my saving, so I vowed never to reveal my mistake to my parents. But, of course, everyone else did.

My mother broached the subject as she was French braiding my hair. I was seated in a chair with my back to her (we never faced crisis head on), when she said, "I understand that you were called forth in the Baptist Bible School."

I began to cry. "I didn't know," I choked out miserably.

Mom's hand released of a section of my hair, an unprecedented act on her part, and she patted me on the shoulder. "It was a misunderstanding, but I've explained to the Reverend that you are not a Baptist." She resumed braiding and continued to explain that I would be properly saved when I turned twelve-years-old and was baptized in the Disciples of Christ Christian Church. My sins would just have to hang in there until that time. It was a mixed blessing, to be sure.

And so it was, at this early age I began to doubt the fickle salvation of God Almighty in the conflicting hands of his hired help.

HOME ON THE RANGE

JUDITH PORTER

"SEE THIS?" DAD HELD UP a bottle of Heinz 57 Sauce and pointed to it. "That's us. Fifty-seven varieties. And none of them Indian."

Every year my brother and I came home from school with a mimeographed slip of paper for my parents to sign—the amount of Native American blood in our family. Our school got extra money according to this proportion. My disappointment was being one of the few flat-liners on the percentage scale.

We lived in an oil camp in northern Oklahoma, where there was nothing much but a few houses and oil.

In the 1940s and '50s life was pretty basic. Our family didn't talk much. Conversations around the dining room table mostly revolved around the food spread before us.

"Hot luv, you make a mean biscuit," Dad would say to Mom. "You have a knack with lard and baking powder."

Occasionally Dad had some words of wisdom to share that were not about food. In further thoughts on the subject of our ethnicity, for instance, he explained that we were, "A little bit of this, a little bit of that."

Our forebears meandered into Oklahoma from every which way. Texas, Alabama, Tennessee, Iowa. "You'd need a road map to trace our ancestry," my dad liked to say.

We were tried and true Okies, as was our food. Perhaps that's why I never heard words like pasta, pizza, taco, tofu or fondue. The only ethnic foods I knew were goulash and French toast.

Food, however, was our family's common ground.

We were beef eaters. After all, we lived in the middle of cow country. Pot roast, hamburgers, chicken fried steak, T-bone steak, bar-b-que, rib-eye. Bring it on.

My dad and most other male relatives were hunters. Rabbit, squirrel, venison, quail, duck, and frogs were a regular part of our diet. Hunting wasn't just a sport. We ate what was bagged. It went like this: hunt, kill, gut, skin, butcher, cook, and on the table in time for supper.

I learned early on how to skin rabbits and squirrels, scale fish, and pluck every kind of bird imaginable. I also learned how to avoid buckshot so as not to break a tooth.

My dad was king of the condiments. A circle in the center of the table was reserved for his Heinz 57 Sauce, A1 Sauce, Ketchup, Mustard, Tabasco sauce, home-made bar-b-que sauce, and vinegar. Dad's personal philosophy was that practically any vegetable could be enhanced with vinegar, especially spinach, cabbage, cauliflower, and cucumbers. After all, Mom had a tendency to cook all vegetables into a tender mush and serve them with salt and pepper. Vinegar was decidedly helpful.

A lot of our meals were fried. There was no other way to cook chicken or fish as far as I knew. The only fish we ever had were catfish from Dad's trotline or pond perch. And fried was the only way they tasted okay.

On slack days we ate chipped beef from a jar with white sauce (shit on a shingle). And, of course, beans. We ate navy beans, pork 'n beans, cowboy beans, pinto beans, and black eyed peas and hominy. Beans were served with applesauce and cornbread, naturally.

And always fresh tomatoes. Peeled and sliced. It was a known fact, according to my mom, that there was no meal on earth that couldn't be improved with sliced tomatoes.

At some point when I was an early teen, my dad took up cooking. He said it was self-defense.

He started cutting out recipes from the Tulsa World newspaper. He made things called cacciatore, tetrazzini, lasagna, and stroganoff, words foreign to us. Even Dad would sometimes have trouble pronouncing them, having only read, not heard them.

He had this huge bowl. It was rough pottery on the out-side with a lime green ceramic glaze on the inside. I don't know where he found it. This was the Fifties when no one had lime green anything, except maybe a lime.

The bowl would be filled with layer after layer of colors—red, green, white, orange, brown, all affection-ately covered with sauces and topped with some yellow or white cheese that would melt and ooze all the way to the bottom. His reputation spread as the gourmet of Carter Nine, Oklahoma.

He experimented with rattlesnake.

He developed a loving relationship with tongue and ox tail.

I should say that it was understood that we eat all parts of the animal, including organs. Liver and onions were a mainstay.

I remember going to a sleepover at a girlfriend's ranch where we were served fried mountain oysters (calf testicles) for breakfast.

However, I balked when my dad handed me a plate of brains and eggs one morning. The brains looked like, well, brains.

"I'll have a piece of toast."

Dad was not happy. "Those brains will probably enhance your own mind," he suggested.

"Those are cow brains. Cows are the dumbest creatures alive. They aren't likely to enhance any part of me."

I did, however have a favorite animal organ: the chicken gizzard.

While we rarely went out to eat—there was no place to go, we did occasionally dine at a fried chicken restaurant when we visited my grandparents in Arkansas. Because they served only chicken, the menu included a platter full of fried gizzards. I was in heaven.

If there was conversation at the table with the family, I was not privy to it. My jaws were masticating gristle, which took all my attention.

Speaking of my grandparent's farm, this is where my dad decided he needed to slaughter a pig. He helped kill it and butcher it into the various parts, bacon, pork chops, ribs, roast. He made spam from some recipe he found. He cured some pieces for ham. He cleaned the guts and used an old fashioned contraption to fill the cleaned gut with his home-made sausage recipe. Somehow we all survived.

When I was twenty-two I got married. It didn't take. My husband was from Chicago and thought he knew more about food than I did. I let him know I was quite adept at cooking. After all, I could make shit on a shingle and tuna casserole, thank you very much. "And, by the way," I said. "Where's your gun?"

We had three children before we parted. They seem relatively normal.

My daughter takes after her grandfather in that she, too is obsessed with food and is actively original in her cooking. But she's on a different plane when it comes to her diet choices. She is part of the new age where experimentation involves vegan, gluten free, and detoxing juices.

She recently says to me, "I don't eat nightshades," and I'm thinking, well, neither do I. Or anybody else, for that matter. But she's talking about the food group nightshades, consisting of tomatoes, among other things. And immediately I can see my mom turning over in her grave (thank goodness she was cremated). Tomatoes were sacred to our early life, like Protestantism or square dancing. What has happened to this family heritage?

I do not understand how we can have these dramatic divisions. We are of the same blood. Granted, my youth was more bloody than most, but still. My line shouldn't have created a vegan grandson and a daughter who, as my dad would say, went every which way with her culinary choices. Every which way, that is, but our way.

JUST THE TWO OF US

JUDITH PORTER

I SAT IN THE FRONT SEAT of our Studebaker on that June day in 1955. I was eleven years old, headed to visit my girlfriend who lived in Kansas while my dad visited refineries for Skelly Oil Company. Today kids my age would be in the back seat locked in a seatbelt. Not so back then. I was right up front with my dad.

He was wearing short-sleeved shirt and slacks—probably khakis. That's what he usually wore. He was bald, but he might have been wearing his hat. If he didn't have it on, it was in the back seat. He didn't go anywhere without his brimmed hat. His hairy left arm was on the windowsill. I could see his tattoo JP. He'd done that to himself, with a straight blade razor and dark ink. He was quick to point out to us that it was a stupid decision he had made as a kid, and now he had to live with the crude results.

There weren't many other distinguishing characteristics about my dad. He'd once been a good-looking man, but when you're a kid, you don't think of your dad as handsome, especially when he's bald and has a big belly.

We were in Udall, Kansas, staring out at the utter devastation from the tornado that had ripped through the town on May 25, just a week or so before.

"Over 70 people died here," Daddy said. He pulled the car up to the curb. "Look at that filling station." He shook his head and puffed on a cigarette. "That thing's made out of cinder blocks. Ripped apart."

I looked around. Almost all the buildings were in shambles. If any tree stood, it had no leaves. Everything felt brown.

Why was he showing me this? If we were sharing a father daughter moment, it escaped my understanding. I was already too familiar with tornadoes considering the many times we ran to our storm cellar as rain and hail pounded down on us.

Lightning. Thunder. The cellar itself. A deep hole carved into the ground with wooden boards for the floor and seats. Dark, damp, water pooling in the bottom. My fears of these horrific storms were already deeply imbedded.

Yet here we were, just the two of us, caged inside a car, looking out the windows at something unspeakable.

My dad and I didn't do much together. When he had spare time, he liked to fish, hunt, smoke and drink. I didn't do any of those things. We were misfits.

My brother, on the other hand, was my dad's pride and joy. He hunted, fished, mastered the bow and arrow, played football. He did all the right stuff.

My dad and my brother understood each other.

I was the girl.

There was another reason my dad and I danced around each other, never quite connecting. He had a lifelong commitment to booze. It's been said that daughters of alcoholics try to be perfect to avoid difficult situations. They have to maintain control over behavior and feelings. My conduct was a little bit along those lines.

I went to college although my dad wasn't enthusiastic about the idea. I majored in journalism because he majored in journalism. He never graduated. I did.

I remember once when he visited me on the campus. He'd been on a business trip to Oklahoma City and stopped by Norman. At the time I was one of two people up for a journalism award. That evening was a banquet where the winner would be announced. "Well, I'll stay if you think you're gonna win," he said. I didn't think I was going to win, and I told him so. I could have said I wanted him there and he probably would have stayed, but then he might have seen me lose and I didn't want that. And he wanted to go home. So we said goodbye. He went to Tulsa and I won the award. He almost saw me accomplish something special.

Daddy, however, was more interested in me being married than he was in my education. He wanted me settling down in my own home with my own family. It didn't quite work out the way he thought it should, but I did marry.

I clearly remember my dad walking me down the aisle. He was trying to be cool, but I had the feeling he wanted a stiff drink of bourbon to get him through. Mom read him the riot act about not taking a drink before the ceremony. His hands were shaking as he held my arm. His legs were wobbly. I could feel his knees knocking. I wasn't sure which of us was holding the other up.

We made it through.

He said to me, "Just remember that once you're married you don't come home again. You take care of your own problems and if you have children, you take care of them." I got the message so when I divorced, I never asked for help. My three kids and I struggled, but we managed, even when I went on food stamps to make ends meet. We were on our own.

When he retired he became interested in writing his family history. He did a lot of research, talked to relatives, and compiled a significant document which he sent to family members. I was so excited to get my copy until I read about us. He described my brother as having played Canadian pro football, teaching, and being a high school principal. He described me as an 'administrative assistant.'

"Daddy, why did you say that?" I asked him. "I have four college degrees and I supervise the five libraries in my school department. I'm not a secretary."

He shot back irritably, "I never did understand what the hell you do." He wasn't being unkind. I think his anger was somewhat directed inward. He really didn't know what I did. When he wrote an addendum a year later to correct some mistakes like birthdays, career changes, etc. he didn't correct my occupation.

The smoking and drinking caught up with him when he was in his seventies. He got esophagus cancer. A hole in his throat meant he ceased to be able to eat or drink. A tube was inserted in his side for nourishment.

It was my April vacation from school, so I flew home to spend a week with Mom and visit Dad in the hospital. Inside his rolling table by his bed were his books, and also his cigarettes and lighter. The nurse said he might as well have them if he wanted them. It didn't matter anymore.

But he didn't smoke. He didn't read either. I took one of his pocketbooks—Killer Angels by Michael Sharra, about the Civil War. My dad was fascinated with American historical books. I liked to read but would not have picked this one out on my own. I was interested to see what interested him and I loved the book.

We didn't have any of those long truthful talks. We had meaningless sporadic conversations when friends and relatives dropped by to visit. Mostly I kept my nose in the book for all the silences that filled the week.

I don't know why my brother wasn't there, but it was just my mom and me. On the last day of my vacation we went to the hospital for me to say goodbye. When we arrived on his floor, the nurses looked grim. They pulled us aside and told us what had happened. My dad had taken the trusty lighter they left in the drawer and burned every tube attached to him. Then he got out of bed and headed down the hall. He'd had enough of hospital care. They caught him, of course, and now he was back in his bed. Mom stayed behind to do some paperwork, but I went to his room.

He was tied down. His waist, legs, even his arms were tethered to the bed. Only his eyes moved. He stared at me and I stared back. Here we were, each caged in our own way. Just the two of us, once again facing the unspeakable.

THE WAR BETWEEN US

JUDITH PORTER

T HE DISTANCE BETWEEN OUR LIVES and our dreams tends to diverge beyond what we imagine. My dream of marriage, for instance, did not turn out as I thought it would.

My husband and I married while we were both in college. He was a NESEP (Naval Enlisted Scientific Education Program). This officially made me a military wife, although I had no concept of the term. He was in the Navy. I had seen the Atlantic Ocean twice as a child. We lived in land-locked Oklahoma attending the University of Oklahoma.

We had a baby that first year of marriage, and then, with only one semester to complete his degree, my husband decided he hated engineering and quit college.

The Navy was not pleased.

No longer officer material, he immediately received orders to Vietnam. He left me and our baby and went to this strange land where conflict was becoming more extensive. He lived in a tent, ate canned WWII C-rations, and worked with amphibious crafts. Though not directly in combat, he was living and working in a war zone and knew the feeling of bullets whirring past his head.

I knew nothing about the war. This was 1966, long before the peace symbols, protest marches, flower children, and Kent State.

It was a war that was happening someplace else to someone else. Not us. Neither my family nor friends talked about the conflict.

While Frank was in Vietnam, I remained on the campus, working on a second degree.

I put our recently purchased early American furniture in storage and moved to the married students' stucco apartments on Sooner Drive. My new place was on the first floor, making easy access to the swing set and sand box right out the kitchen door. The apartment had blond college-issue institutional furniture. I hadn't given it much thought at the time, but I realize now, that I had stored away all vestiges of my married life and was starting anew.

I was a war wife although I had no concept of that role. I kept my life and my baby Lee's life in a simple routine: I went to classes; she went to nursery school. We often spent weekends in Tulsa with my parents. Mom loved to pamper my daughter. My dad liked cooking steaks on the grill. I could relax and study.

I developed a friendship with two men in the student union cafeteria. I don't remember how we met, but we were an odd trio. One was Asian and the other a Mormon. I was a young mother. We would meet for lunch several times a week. Our different backgrounds provided lively conversations.

Our friendship, however, did not extend beyond the walls of that cafeteria. That is, until one night when I received a phone call from the Asian. He was frightened.

I listened as he explained how his wife had just had a baby and she couldn't get the baby to nurse. The baby was howling in the background and I remember thinking how hard this must be for such a private man with obvious cultural differences to be forced to relate such an intimate issue to a woman acquaintance. I don't believe his wife spoke English. Their whole family was back in China.

It just so happened that I, too, had difficulty nursing my baby, so I actually knew what to say to him. I explained how I had handled the situation and reassured him that if she, indeed, could not nurse, they could easily resort to bottled formula and the baby would still thrive.

I surprised myself at how mature I had handled our conversation. Words flowed freely. He seemed genuinely grateful for my help.

We never discussed this again, other than for him to tell me his wife was doing well and so was the baby.

I was not as mature in dealing with my absent husband.

I wrote letters and waited to hear back from him. Correspondence was sparse. When he did write, the letters were somewhat mundane. He told of going into the village occasionally to teach English to villagers. He added that he didn't know if those same young people were also snipers attacking them at night. I would write back about our daughter's development in this first year of her life. There wasn't much more to tell him.

I watched the news give war reports on our black and white television set. I scanned the faces of the men, wondering if I would see the one I knew.

I survived that year by keeping a safe distance from actually thinking about what was going on across the Pacific Ocean.

I didn't realize it then, but this was the first time I had truly been on my own. I had gone from a childhood of parental authority, to dorm life on campus where I felt like everyone was watching me (which they weren't), to marriage (love and obey). Now, suddenly, I had a taste of true independence, which included organizing a budget and making decisions and for me and my baby. It was a newfound freedom. I liked it.

The year passed quickly.

I was studying for finals one Sunday afternoon when I got a phone call from Frank. "I'm in Dallas," he said.

I didn't understand. His voice was much too clear. The few other phone calls I had received in the past months were some sort of short-wave radio where I had to say, "over" when I finished talking. Primitive and impersonal conversations.

My mind was trying to figure out how Dallas got in Vietnam.

"Dallas," he said again. "Texas. I'll be home in two hours."

My textbooks and papers were strewn all over the floor, along with Lee's toys. It was final exams week and I was studying furiously. I hadn't washed my hair, cleaned up the house, or shopped in a while. Everything was a mess.

His unexpected announcement left me with only two frantic hours to pull my life together and drive to the airport to welcome my husband home from Vietnam. Unfortunately, I also had an important final examination scheduled for eight o'clock the following morning.

I called my professor. "My husband is back from Vietnam two months early." And he said, "So?"

I had no answer to that.

"He's been gone all year. I haven't seen him," I stumbled on. "He's been in the Vietnam war. I, I, can't take my exam in the morning. I can't be ready."

He said nothing.

I cried.

The professor, no doubt anxious to get this hysterical woman off the phone, quickly said I could come to his office and take the exam at one o'clock instead of the scheduled morning time. I had a five-hour reprieve.

I cried some more, not because this man had no idea why I was upset about my husband's return from war, but I cried for me. I wasn't ready to have my husband home in the middle of finals and I hated myself for reacting this way.

I put on a Jackie Kennedy pink suit, combed my oily hair and washed and dressed our toddler before driving to the Will Rogers's Airport in Oklahoma City.

My war hero stood on the curb with a duffle bag that looked equal in size to what was left of his thin frame. He was like a shadow of the man I married. His hair was nearly shaved off and his uniform was wrinkled. Everything reeked of something from the swamp.

I opened the door and smiled, tears streaming down both cheeks. He gave me a kiss, hugging me tightly until a tiny voice called from the front seat. "Mama?"

"Here's your daughter," I said.

Frank leaned over, peeking into the window and grinned. Lee drew back.

I unlocked the trunk so he could lift the duffel bag inside. I climbed back behind the wheel as Frank settled in the seat beside me, drawing Lee onto his lap. From a paper sack he pulled a teddy bear for her and a pair of gold earrings for me. He got them both at the Dallas airport.

Lee was silent as she sat on his lap holding her stuffed bear and trying to connect this smelly strange man with the word, "Daddy."

Once home, I insisted that Frank leave the duffel bag on the porch because the mildew odor was so overwhelming.

Our conversation came in bolts and starts and halted in painful silences.

I had the reverse argument with my husband that I had with my professor when I tried to explain why I had to take my exam the next afternoon. I had to prepare for it. He didn't like that. I wasn't the same person he remembered.

It was not a momentous reception.

I had trouble putting Lee to bed that evening. I had to sing three songs and read two books while Frank stood in the doorway.

He wouldn't undress. Just paced back and forth. Finally, he said, "Foot fungus."

"What?" My eyes immediately fell to his feet. His combat boots looked like they had melted.

"That's what you probably smell. Foot fungus. Everyone gets it." I started to say, 'don't take them off,' but I stopped myself. This was his home. He should be able to take off a pair of boots.

I backed away, waiting for gnarled toes or black wrinkled heels. Something dreadful and disgusting. But they weren't so bad. Red, chapped, wilted like wet lettuce.

That's when I made the mistake of laughing. All the pent-up fears came out in guffaws and gasps as I held my sides and let tears flow freely down my face.

Frank stared at me without speaking.

We were different people than the ones who had parted the year before.

There were other things.

We didn't discuss his experience. I was partly trying to stay in the cocoon I had built around myself. I didn't want to know.

He brought a grotesque souvenir of a dried fish shaped into a human form—head, legs, arms. He tried numerous ways to relieve the piece of its foul fishy odor, so I would accept it and, I don't know, hang it on some wall? I balked until he gave in and threw it away. I think he really liked that thing.

And so much more came between us.

There were many heroes during that war. I was not one of them. I'm not proud of my behavior when he returned. I was not the same wife anymore. Self-sufficient. Defiant.

We had both lived with anxiety for a year and our lives moved in different directions. It wasn't good for anybody.

We stayed together for a few more years and two more children before divorcing and going our separate ways. Still, that single quiet year has stayed with me and sustained me through many future hard times.

VOICE OF A VINTAGE VOLVO

Judith Porter

"**Y**OU DRIVE LIKE MARIO ANDRETTI," the man said to my owner and I could tell it made her a little proud to hear this. She'd picked up this sailor at the NATO base and was giving him a lift to the port. It was a pretty common practice to give rides to sailors trying to get back to their ships while faced with less than predictable bus service.

Anyway, she'd been breezing along through traffic when she downshifted and the whole damn gear shaft came off in her hand. Didn't faze her a bit. By that time, she was as comfortable with me and my quirks as I was with her and hers. She just stuck the pole back in the slot and shifted again, not missing a beat. The poor sailor didn't fare as well. His eyes bugged out and he grabbed my dashboard and gritted his teeth. When she dropped him off, he smiled and thanked her for the ride, but I could see he was a wee bit scared. I think that pleased her.

I was a red Volvo sedan of indeterminable age. I'm not good with numbers, but I did know this was 1967, and she and her husband spent $450 for me. I'd been around for several years, shuffled between military families assigned to overseas duty in Naples, Italy. She called me an oldie but goodie, which I thought was a pretty accurate description.

She didn't like cars, she told her friend Helen while we were driving around. When she took driver's education in high school she was clumsy and nervous, so she didn't take the exam for a license until a year later. Besides, she lived in rural Oklahoma where the roads were long and flat with an occasional unexpected curve or intersection, resulting in some loss of friends. There was Johnny and Joe, both killed in a head on crash coming home from Ponca City. And Dale. Dale, a lifelong buddy, was supposed to meet her brother that night, but never arrived. They found him in a ditch the next day.

When she did start driving in Tulsa, she was returning home from work at the soda fountain driving her dad's Studebaker when it was sideswiped by a guy who ran a stop sign. She started her freshman year at Oklahoma University wearing a neck brace. Cars scared her.

But when I came along, things changed. Her husband was stationed on board a ship that was out to sea all but about three or four days a month, so she was on her own in a strange land. Thanks to the military wives assigning a buddy to help her adjust, she met Helen and the fun began.

Helen became her best friend and constant companion. Helen, however, didn't even know how to drive a car, so my owner was the chauffeur. Despite her deficiency behind the wheel, Helen had been in Naples almost two years and had scouted the area. Together the two women ventured anywhere and everywhere with me. They went into the heart of Naples to check out Shoe Alley or Nativity Alley or the Flower Market. They combed the city for adventure, often getting lost in the process.

It was crazy on the streets of Naples. Those little three-wheeled vehicles were everywhere, darting in and out, and often going right up on the sidewalks. My owner said that if Italians didn't have their horns to play with while driving, she didn't know what they would do. It was pure chaos when you got onto the roads in Naples. I already knew this, having been on the streets for years, but it was all new to her.

Every misadventure offered a new challenge and she accepted it with gusto. I remember one time when she drove into a center of several converging streets and found us in the middle of many cars with angry drivers honking and signaling for her to get out of the way. There was, of course, nowhere to go since we were blocked in, and those Italians knew it. But she was the American female and they thought they were putting her in her place. She and Helen were laughing themselves silly because neither spoke the language and there was a whole lot of language going on around us. Finally, she solved the problem by turning off my engine, pulling the keys out of the keyhole, and holding them up in the air outside the window. That was her way of saying, "We're not going anywhere. This is up to you!" And you know what? Everyone backed up and moved aside so we could drive on.

In June, 1967, when the attack on the *USS Liberty* occurred in the Sinai Peninsula, her husband's ship, the *Sylvania,* set off to try to supply the damaged vessel. All the wives living in Naples were terrified. We picked up Helen and went to the NATO base to meet with other wives for a conference about the situation. The combined air and sea attack had killed 34 crew members and wounded 171 on the Liberty, as well as severely damaging the ship. There was talk of war for several days, so the atmosphere was somber. The *Sylvania* was unable to get close enough to the injured ship to assist them, so they turned back to the more stable waters of the Mediterranean. It took a while, but eventually, things returned to less serious events.

Helen knew places to see and was a good map reader. My owner, with rapidly gaining confidence, was raring to go anywhere. During the almost three years she lived in Naples we ventured out of the city, traveling to Caserta to the Royal Palace, Paestum to the Greek ruins, the coast of Amalfi, the volcanic ruins of Pompeii.

The Lily Festival in Nola was pretty amazing. A hundred and twenty men shouldered each one of the giant Gigli, parading throughout the town. Gigli were large wooden obelisks measuring eighty-two feet high and shaped as intricate lilies. It was a site to behold.

Still, one of their favorite trips took us to Otaviano to the bottle factory. They watched as big green bottles were blown into shape and then they purchased several in different sizes. Her daughter Jeannette Lee had to sit on Helen's lap for the drive home since they filled my back seat and trunk with bottles.

Often on the winding roads, we would find ourselves blocked by herds of sheep. Once there was a large cart being drawn by an ox. My owner said there was nothing to do but get out of the car and take a photograph while waiting for them to pass. So that's what she did.

She loved the scenery in the countryside. The vineyards, for instance, strung the grape vines all the way up between tall trees.

Meanwhile, these were turbulent times back in the United States, wherever that was. I was Scandinavian and had never been there, so I wasn't too informed. But I listened to the discussions that often included terrible things happening. In April 1968, Martin Luther King Jr. was assassinated, and in June, Robert F. Kennedy was shot, too. In August, violence, political turbulence, and civil unrest surrounded the Democratic National Convention in Chicago.

My owner and Helen had trouble getting additional facts because they had no television, telephone, or newspaper. Their only source of information was a Monday through Friday, fifteen-minute radio news broadcast in English. On a lighter note, in January of 1969, Joe Namath and the New York Jets were the first AFL team to win the Super Bowl. My owner was an Okie and liked that stuff.

1968 was also when my owner was pregnant. Early one morning in late November her water broke. She wasn't sure what that meant, and she couldn't call the hospital and ask since there was no phone. So, she cleaned up the house, changed the sheets, then walked Lee over to a friend in the next building to babysit. She packed a little suitcase and a bottle of calamine lotion because Lee had just come down with chickenpox. Then the two of us went to the hospital.

She went inside and said her water broke but she had no contractions so should she stay? The nurse said she should get off her feet immediately. She decided not to mention to the nurse that she'd driven me out to Pozzuoli where the hospital was located and left me in the parking lot. She delivered her baby within two hours.

Her husband, of course, was out to sea. He returned a week later, but not to see the new baby boy. His mother had committed suicide in Chicago, and he was headed back to the states.

She and I were left in charge of Christmas that year. She'd pack that newborn in a carrier with Jeannette Lee beside him and off we went to buy a Christmas tree and stuff it in my trunk and pick up the layaway presents. We also mailed packages back home and bought food for the holiday dinner. Her husband showed up on Christmas Eve, in time to help assemble some of the toys: a dollhouse and some other things. The family made it through, but it wasn't exactly joyous.

Before we knew it, New Year's Eve rolled around. That was my most dreaded holiday of the year. In Naples, at the stroke of midnight, the tradition was 'out with the old and in with the new.' Everything and anything that was unwanted went over the balconies and crashed onto the ground or road below. I was terrified of getting dented or crushed. After all, it was not uncommon to see a refrigerator come flying over a balcony. And lots of Christmas trees came down, some even flaming.

My owner moved me to a higher location so I wouldn't be in the line of fire, for which I was grateful. Smoke filled the area with all the fireworks going on, but I could still see her standing on the balcony watching the activity and keeping a worried eye on me. She was taking care of me, just as I had been trying my best to take care of her. After all, we were a team.

MY BROTHER JUDD

JUDITH PORTER

OR YOU, DEATH WAS IMMEDIATE and final. For the rest of us, your death lingered in increments that endure to this day.

It was March 2010, when Mom and I made that flight to Ashville, North Carolina, for your funeral. It was the longest trip of my life. Mom's, too. Even longer for her. You were her fist born, her son, the pride and joy.

I was seated beside her. Alive. Your little sister.

Mom couldn't live without you and passed away just a few months later.

Your funeral was a nightmare. Mom and I stayed in your house, but the trophy wife made sure we knew it was no longer your house. She had it all.

Your daughter raised hell over not doing an autopsy. We were all at odds over so many things. One of the trophy's sons has a seizure and we had to call 911. She had her friends come to sit with Mom to make sure she didn't any steal paintings off the walls.

Food arrived in carloads: casseroles, potato salads, macaroni salads, corn bread, hams, cakes and cookies. The kitchen counters were strewn with cellophane and aluminum foil covering half eaten contributions from neighbors and teachers.

The trophy decided to have you embalmed for a viewing before having you cremated. I asked her why she would do both?

She said, "Oh you know us Okies. Someone dies and you gotta have a casket and a casserole."

I was so angry at you. I sat on the floor in your closet, surrounded by your oversized clothes, picking through, piece by piece, everything in your safe, trying to find some hint that you had, indeed, left a will. You were already weary of this third wife, and you had no patience with her 'lay about' sons. Yet, here she was with all your possessions.

All I wanted was your dog because I knew how much you loved him, and I was worried about his fate. I didn't get him, which was just as well. He would have terrorized my cats. He was a shelter mutt, but he looked to me like a tree walker coon hound mix.

You insisted on getting his DNA tested. I remember the delight in your voice when you called to announce, "He's a Chihuahua!"

Animals and nature were as much a part of your life as cars and college degrees.

We had a special childhood, growing up in the country. Mom and Dad let us keep most of the critters you caught and dragged home.

Except the hawk. Dad wouldn't let you keep him when Mom refused to hang out the laundry with a hawk perched on the clothesline pole.

You were the bird watcher, the snake charmer, the insect collector.

You taught me many useless things, like how to syphon gas from the tractors and trucks in the farm fields. You and your friends had gotten that infamous orange car, held together with chewing gum and duct tape, but you were always short on cash for fuel.

We had fun announcing that you wore size twelve shoes when you were twelve-years-old. You kept growing to keep up with your feet. In college, I wanted you to go bowling with me, but we'd walk into a bowling alley and ask, "what's the biggest shoe you rent?" knowing it was not going to be size 15 ½.

You topped out at almost six foot seven inches tall, fifty-one inches across the shoulders. We thought you were larger than life, which is probably why we couldn't believe you could die.

It seemed like you filled a room when you entered, with both your size and incredible sense of humor. You were the storyteller, yet I am left behind to try to piece together your story.

Your first wife was a sweet country girl, but she just couldn't keep up with you. I remember that Valentine's day when she called me to say you'd disappeared. I went down to Paul's Valley to stay with her. She said you drove off to work but never arrived and never called the school. Later that evening you phoned from somewhere deep in Texas to say you thought maybe you'd come back home.

You arrived with two heart shaped boxes of chocolates. I suggested that it was a hell of a long way to go for Valentine chocolates.

"They were on sale," you replied.

Your second wife was a gem and mother of your two children. But you just had to have that third, the trophy. What a piece of work she turned out to be.

You would have hated that she didn't honor your wishes and she cut your children and grandchildren out of their inheritance. You were supposed to be the smart one, but without leaving a will, you failed in this life lesson.

You were the educator, serving almost a dozen schools in the states and Canada. An innovator. A mover and a shaker. And I might mention, given your size, discipline was never much of an issue. You had many accomplishments in education, including runner up for Principal of the Year of North Carolina.

The Trophy jumped on the Internet and came up with a new husband within a year. She sold the house, loaded all your stuff, and moved to Georgia. She did drop off some boxes in Oklahoma of unwanted items that had belonged to you: yearbooks, awards, certificates, your office memorabilia.

From that lot I received the walking stick that was carved for you by one of the teachers at Ashville High School. It was presented to you when you retired. On it was this saying by O.S. Card:

The bigger the man is the more people he serves
A small man serves himself
Bigger is to serve your family
Bigger is to serve your tribe
Then your people
Biggest of all is to serve all men
And all lands.

R.I.P. Big Brother

BROWN BAG OF CANDY

BROWN BAG OF CANDY

Janet Skinner

I DON'T REMEMBER MOVING INTO 64 Mead Avenue, but I could tell from the old photos of clam bakes in the back yard and Easter pictures taken in our holiday finery, the place wasn't in very good shape when we moved in. The house's back yard was almost directly across the street from my parent's former apartment. Dad bought the house without Mom having much to say about it. It cost $7000. I can remember stroller rides down to the local hardware store to make cash payments to the owner, who held the mortgage. Dad hated debt and paid the house off well before the due date, by working two jobs.

Mom did not like the house. She had her reasons. The house was large, old fashioned, built around the turn of the century. A working- class two family, without central heating, it needed painting, both inside and out. The yard hadn't been touched in years.

Worse, the bathrooms had old faded white claw foot tubs. Taking a shower presented a challenge: connect the rubber hose -shower head attachment to the spigot in the tub, adjust the flow and temperature of the hot/cold mixture holding the shower head above you as you sat in the tub, then try to shower, scrubbing simultaneously. Baths in the second-floor warm bathroom were much easier. In winter, fill the tub with very hot water. close the door tightly, allow the room to warm with steam, then wash up, dry off quickly, race into your pajamas, run like hell down to the first floor to stand near the grate from which the coal heat emanated. My youngest brother once, toddling around, accidentally fell and was branded with the grate pattern on his thigh. Pet painted turtles (we each had one) were not allowed anywhere near the grate, although one somehow escaped my brother's clutches. It fell through, dying in the inferno.

The coal-fired furnace needed to be fed regularly, so temperatures varied depending upon the time of the day. At bedtime, we'd all fall asleep under heavy layers of woolen blankets while Dad would descend to the earthen cellar to bank the fire, keeping the embers going until morning. Then, getting up before six, he would return to shovel in coal, so we awoke to a semblance of warmth. To allow the heat from the first floor to move up into the second floor, he had cut two one-foot square holes in the ceiling. The rising heat from the first floor heated the second floor. The third floor was always cold.

Probably the earliest memory I had of the old house was watching Dad work in vegetable garden, whistling away like he always did when picking tomatoes. I sat in warm, soapy water, getting a bath in the large kitchen sink, right near the open back door. It was summer; no heat required.

I was fascinated by the coal delivery man and his wonderful silver slide. Backing his truck into our driveway, he'd open the cellar window right above the coal bin. The window was just wide enough to allow him to insert the slide around the corner of the truck, through the window, into the bin. This slide seemed magical to me. Shining brighter silver, smoother, more slippery and fast than any I'd seen at the play- ground, I'd watch from the cellar stairs, as he cascaded shovel after shovel of the black, glossy rocks down into the bin. Without looking, he knew just when the receptacle was full.

I had always dreamed of taking a swift ride down that slide, navigating the corner, soft- landing right into the middle of the full black pile. Thank God it never happened.

Eventually we got oil heat. I don't know why. Maybe it was an effort to appease Mom.

My beloved Grandma Jenny and her second husband Pat moved into the apartment on the second and third floor right after she was diagnosed with multiple sclerosis. For some reason, perhaps, because of her illness or the loss of Pat's leg in an explosion at his work, Pat had his bedroom on the third floor. Going up to his room in the early morning, I'd trip over the toe of his big clunky wooden right leg, forgetting that it came off at night. He always tucked it neatly under the bed frame, part way sticking out, the shoe and sock still on it. I also remember that when he walked, wearing the leg, it would creak and groan while he huffed and puffed with each step. Maneuvering the heavy leg was an effort to defy gravity. The recalcitrance of the wooden limb that was supposed to be a support, often seemed to me more like a burden, although he never complained.

There was a great open space in our backyard, right below Grandma Jenny's back porch where two of my brothers and I made a fort.

In the final stages of her multiple sclerosis, Grandma was unable to navigate the stairs but would watch us from above. Always as if by magic or heavenly angels, a brown paper bag, lowered on a long white string would appear full of candy. Grandmother was our heavenly magic, letting us know that she was there, in our lives.

She died in the bedroom directly above mine, I was only 6 years old, but remember her silent, pale figure in bed, as if it were yesterday.

SOKOL EXPERIENCE

JANET SKINNER

I T WAS WEDNESDAY NIGHT. AFTER finishing supper with my mom and dad, my brothers and I climbed into out gym uniforms, a tee shirt over shorts. The shorts had elastic threaded through the hem so the leg opening fit snuggly about the upper thigh.

The Sokol Gymnastic Union was about a quarter of a mile from our house. Walking or sometimes running if we were behind schedule, we didn't want to be late or we would catch the wrath of our Uncle Rog, the head coach.

We lived in Byram, a Slovak ghetto, of sorts, in the southern part of the wealthy town of Greenwich, Connecticut. The village was populated primarily by immigrants, who at the turn of the century had been hired directly from the old country to work in the local foundry. We were the grand children of one of those men.

Like most ethnic groups new to this country, a fraternal club and a church were ways to have one foot in America and the other in the homeland. The Slovak Lutheran Church, whose Pastor had sponsored most of the recent arrivals, had services in both Slovak and English.

It was at the Sokol Club where I learned both the national anthem of the United States, and (sung in Slovak) that of Slovakia. Both anthems were sung at the large competitive gymnastic meets held once a year called Slets. Gymnasts from as far away as Pittsburgh would practice set routines on various apparatus. The culmination of the competition was a performance of hundreds of gymnasts equally spaced apart on a large field, doing calisthenics to music in unison.

Arriving at the club, my brothers and I separated. I went into the girl's dressing room, took off my shoes to put on my gym slippers. Made in Slovakia, they were black canvas uppers, held in place by a strong elastic, with soft suede leather soles which provided "feel" and prevented sliding off apparatus like the balance beam or vaulting horse. They were required as protection from burns and bruises.

We twenty girls had to line up "properly." Facing the center of the gym, we'd extend our left arm out at the shoulder to provide enough space in the line so as not to impinge on our neighbor's movements during calisthenics. Bumping into each other would raise Rog's wrath.

After we girls finished our floor routines, low balance beam, parallel bars and vaulting horse, the teenage boys would commandeer the gym. Bobby was lined up next to Donny and Kenny. The three were the epitome of physical perfection, young, strong, muscular. Practicing the "iron cross" on still rings, suspended by a ring in each hand, they would hang in the shape of a crucified figure on a cross, without anything holding them up, just the strength of their arms. Once each had a turn, they would move to the horizontal bar and try to outdo each other. Jumping up, grabbing hold, swinging rhythmically back and forth, building up speed until they circumnavigated the bar in a complete three- hundred -and -sixty degree rotation. If they generated enough momentum, they could do more than one. Letting go at just the right moment, they'd fly through the air, landing perfectly on their feet, heels together, knees bent, arms out-stretched.

I, on the other hand, was able to manage a respectable effort on the low balance beam, rings, vaulting horse and parallel bars.

At the end of the night we were ordered to again line up. Our coaches stood before us, gave us a little pep talk about our performance that night then in Slovak yell "Dismissed!"

We immediately ran downstairs, threw on our shoes and coats and headed for home. We all knew we'd be back then next week to do it all over again.

We believed that all kids lived as we did.

PLAYLAND

JANET SKINNER

IT STARTED THE FIRST FRIDAY after 4th of July. My brothers and I would search the comic strip page of the local newspaper every day, in anticipation of the fifty percent off coupon that made it affordable for us to have a day of fun at Playland, an amusement park in Rye, New York. Collecting coupons and saving money, we would wait all summer for the Monday of Labor Day weekend to arrive and when it did, we were ready to go.

We'd carefully cut out the coupon, stockpiling them in a special spot in the dining room china cabinet right next to the dragon-painted teapot, the receptacle of any extra cash Mom could spare for our adventure. As the summer dragged on each pile would get bigger, along with our excitement.

For us, clipping coupons and saving money for this special occasion was what you did when you were one of four kids.

Our cousin Gail, who always joined us in this experience, didn't worry at all about money. Everyone pampered her. The golden child, she had lots of things we wished we could have: a new shiny bicycle, pretty new clothes, and a bedroom all her own. We wore hand me downs.

As kids, we didn't understand the family trap that Gail had been born into. We had each other, hostile as it may have gotten at times. But Gail only had Aunt Wilma as her family and best friend.

Arriving at Playland's ticket gate, Dad pulled out our carefully folded coupons, while Mom dug in her handbag and produced the "tea" from her teapot. The ticket seller was impressed with us. "Wow, you got a lot of coupons there, he said. "Lucky today's the last day you can use them." We knew that but acted pleased.

There was an order, a tradition, to how we approached the rides. We didn't just rush around willy-nilly running from ride to ride. We always rode the Turtle Chase first. Climbing up onto the circular seats, perched on the backs of huge turtles, each shell a different color, we'd go around and around, up and down in a huge circular scramble. Gail became more animated, as the turtles went faster and faster. Chasing, unsure of who was chasing whom, we were gleeful in knowing that for yet another year, we'd started the Playland escapade.

At the Carousel, we each jumped onto our favorite horses. I particularly liked the white one, strewn with roses down the mane and tail, and rode it every year. Galloping, lunging forward, while the calliope music played loudly in my ears, I could see Gail, on her dark bay, emblazoned with huge rhinestone diamonds and rubies. Hair flying, shirt flapping as her horse cantered up and down. Not sure of herself, she was holding tightly to the pole that moved the horse, but her face shone with glee.

Leaving the rhythmic and melodic motion of the Carousel, we headed for something a bit more adventuresome and wild. The Whip, across from the Carousel, and just below the roller coaster, had a height requirement. Arriving at the front of the line, we each had to back up against a measuring stick. Too short and you couldn't ride. Gail just made it and beamed.

Snuggling into the cup shaped car, she wedged herself between my two brothers, while I sat with Mom in the car right behind them. Buckling our seat belts, we braced ourselves for take-off. Jerking forward, we tossed back and forth, spinning and careening side to side, laughing hysterically.

The Magic Carpet was a different sort of ride. We sat on a big round circular carpet on rollers, in a room that looked as if it were out of a sultan's harem, as the carpet would start to spin slowly, then pick up speed, going faster and faster. The kids at the edges were the first to go. They were thrown off by the centrifugal force, catapulted onto foam rubber pads along the walls. Once we figured it out, we'd always sit in the middle.

At the end of the day, tradition would dictate the Dragoon Roller Coaster was the last and most fearsome of all our rides. We'd hold our breath looking down at "the whip," while ascending the steep hill we'd anticipated earlier in the day. Entering the cave-like body of the Dragon, we'd exhale and start yelling, as we shot out of the dragon's mouth. Down, down, down the steep swirling decline. Holding on tightly we'd continuing to scream our heads off, as we speed through twists and turns, descending and ascending in rapid succession. Exhilarated, we'd screech to a dead stop, at the exact spot from which we'd started, happy that the brakes worked!

The ride in the car home was pretty quiet, we were all pooped, except for Gail. She chattered away, reliving the best rides of her day. She had become one of us. We were her cousin -friends able to show her how to play, be free, be a kid. In the process we became the "golden children."

STRENGTH

JANET SKINNER

I WAS AT THE KITCHEN SINK, finishing up the supper dishes. Mom had gone upstairs and Dad was out in the yard, working on the rowboat, when the back door flew open and my younger brother Dave came flying in screaming "Toby has been hit by a car." Toby was our five-year old Beagle-Jack Russell mixed breed dog.

We'd had Toby since she was a puppy. Dad carried her home tucked in his jacket after one of his customers gave her to our family. We were overjoyed. We had stopped asking for a dog after the cocker spaniel, adopted from the pound, bit Dave and Mom insisted she be returned.

"What are you talking about?" I barked at him. "She was just here, under my feet. I almost stepped on her." In my opinion, Dave would do anything for attention.

Why would Toby be in the road? Whenever she went out, she was either tied or one of us was with her. But, just to be sure, I headed out the door and down the driveway. I instinctively turned towards my best friend's house because occasionally I'd take Toby there to play with their dog Pepper.

Far down on the sidewalk, I could see a small brown-black body draped listlessly against the edge of the curb. My heart began to pound furiously. I broke into a run. I kept praying, "Maybe Dave made a mistake, no it's not her, please dear God, let it not be her."

A teenage driver stood in the open door of his idling car, staring in disbelief across the hood, at the slumped object near the road. Neither moved.

When I got about 10 feet away, I realized it was Toby. I started wailing, "Toby, Toby!" Then I collapsed in the middle of the sidewalk, my arms wrapped tightly around my shins, my face buried in my knees. I rocked back and forth, groaning.

"Oh no! Oh no!" I repeated. I couldn't get up. I felt like someone had punched me in the gut.

My other brother Bill had followed me out the door and was right on my heels. Leaving me rocking and crying on the sidewalk, he ran past me, scooped up the little limp body and jumped in the teenager's car!

"You are taking me to the vet hospital!" he ordered the driver. Off they sped.

I don't know how long I stayed on the sidewalk, crying, rocking and praying. It seemed like everything was in slow motion. Finally, Mom showed up, got me to my feet and led me home.

In the living room, Mom and I sat in silence, lost in our thoughts and prayers. But, from the top of the stairs we could hear Dave saying to himself, in a loud, angry voice, "Who cares if she dies, she's only a dog!"

Finally, a car pulled into the driveway, and I saw Bill very carefully climb out, gently holding Toby, wrapped in a blanket, her little head sticking out. He placed her carefully on the sofa. She didn't move, but appeared alert, relaxed, knowing she was home.

"She's bruised and scraped, and she was unconscious on the ride to the animal hospital," Billy explained. "But nothing's broken. The vet thinks a few days of TLC and she'll be back to normal." As Toby looked up at him, he gently stroked her head.

The next morning, at the top of the stairs, I found Dave sitting in almost the same position as the day before. He was crying violently, head between his knees, palms cupped over his eyes.

"What's the matter with you?" I demanded.

"I don't want Toby to die." He sobbed between bouts of hyperventilation.

"She's not gonna die." I responded in a matter-of fact tone. "Didn't you hear what Bill said? Only grazed, no damage done... now get out of my way."

I was being the tough big sister, and my brother Dave was being an emotional basket case. But our brother Bill had shown a different side, One I'd never seen before. He had the ability to take charge, a job that was usually mine. Strength, I realized, came in many forms.

I was thankful for it.

ABOUT THE WOMEN OF WRITELIFE

CATHY DEL NERO

Cathy's life is divided into distinct chapters. With degrees in Theatre and English from Tufts University, she focused on acting and directing. A passion for sailing and adventure interrupted. Later, the need for stability bred a surprising thirty-seven-year career as a financial advisor. And now, she is writing. And feels she is home at last.

DIANNE ELLIOTT

Dianne's life, like her careers, has had many iterations. After a short career as an operating room nurse she returned to college to get a B.S. in Nursing and English from Boston College and then a Masters in Mental Health Science from University of California, San Francisco. Her careers, from then forward, included roles as a clinical specialist in Mental Health, an Assistant Hospital Director at Oregon, a Vice President at Swedish Health Services in Seattle and finally owner of her D3 Consulting, an art consulting company specializing in incorporating art as part of a healing environment in healthcare. Throughout this journey, reading and writing kept her sane and centered.

Irene M Hubbard

Irene wrote letters for the first half of her life. As a teen she
 wrote to summer friends all winter long and once married she wrote weekly to her mother-in-law for fifteen years. She always chose Christmas cards that were large and had a lot of blank space so she could write long notes on each card, which she began
doing right after Halloween. Having written so much about her life in this ongoing fashion, she has a fair recollection for memoir writing, which is what she is up to these days. Earlier careers included critical care nursing, family therapy and running a charter sailboat in the Caribbean.

Mary Clare O'Grady

Mary Clare studied at the University of Fribourg, Fribourg,
 Switzerland, received a Bachelor of Science in Finance from Providence College and a Master's in Business Administration from Boston College. After a thirty-five year career in the corporate world, she now spends most days in her studio working on
a novel but can also be found on Aquidneck Island's many walking trails, sipping Earl Grey tea in a local café, or at home gardening or knitting.

JUDITH PORTER

Judith was born and raised in Oklahoma. She holds bach-

elor's degrees in journalism and education from the University of Oklahoma and master's degrees in library science and media services from the University of Rhode Island. For many years she was supervisor of Media Services for the Portsmouth School Department. Since retirement she has both volunteered and been on staff at the Potter League for Animals. Her novel *Coco Twain Tells the Truth* was published in 2005. She is the mother of three and grandmother of six. She lives in Newport with her two cats.

JANET SKINNER

Janet was raised in the village of Byram, in the town of

Greenwich, Connecticut. Graduating from Dental Hygiene school, she later acquired a master's Dental Hygiene Education from Columbia University becoming Clinical Director of Dental Hygiene at the Bristol Community College. Moving to Newport,
she started her own small business, Lily's of the Alley, a woman's boutique. She later received a Master's in Marriage and Family Therapy. Janet continues to work full time in a private practice and as contractor to the Veteran's Administration, seeing military families and individuals. This is her first attempt at writing short memoir stories.

JACK GALVIN

Jack has been a writer and teacher of writing for forty years. With Mark Pfetzer he wrote *Within Reach: My Everest Story* which was honored as an outstanding book for young adults. For many years he was head of the English Department at Rogers High school where he developed and taught composition courses. In summers he was tennis pro at Bailey's Beach and Carnegie Abbey. In addition to his own writing, Jack works as an editor and writing coach.

Made in the USA
Middletown, DE
14 September 2020

19841986R00117